EMPOWERMENT

There is nothing that you cannot do, be, or have

JOHN RANDOLPH PRICE

———

EMPOWERMENT

There is nothing that you cannot do, be, or have

John Randolph Price

Library of Congress Catalog Card Number 92-61916
International Standard Book Number 0-942082-12-5

Published by QUARTUS BOOKS
The Quartus Foundation for Spiritual Research, Inc.
P.O. Box 1768
Boerne, Texas 78006-6768

Printed in the United States of America

Cover art and design by K. Eron Howell

This book is dedicated to the millions of *empowered* men and women who have made the commitment to reveal a new world of love, peace, joy, and abundance—not as a future possibility, but as a present reality to be enjoyed now.

TABLE OF CONTENTS

INTRODUCTION

This book represents many years of searching, discovering, experimenting and measuring the results of the application of certain principles found in Ancient Wisdom Teachings and today's Spiritual Psychology—and then beginning all over again to find the next higher level of working creatively with the Power within. It has been a stimulating adventure of learning and growing, a journey from one state of consciousness to another with a delightful mixture of "fruits" along the way.

I have compared it to a dimensional odyssey, traveling up through dense vibrations of the lower nature—the ego—toward the soaring freedom of the Superconsciousness. In my course of travel there were times when I made the wrong turn, ran into a detour, or got lost in the dark out of ignorance of cosmic principles. On each occasion assistance was provided by the inner Teacher in the form of encouragement, ideas to ponder, study assignments, specific guidance, a divine remedy to try in the laboratory of mind, and in many cases, a bona fide miracle to strengthen my resolve to continue the quest.

Over a period of time my journal was filled with insights, interpretations, research notes, and the result of experimenting with certain spiritual laws of adjustment and correction. *EMPOWERMENT* is the accumulation of much of that material—organized to provide a road map for an exciting spiritual journey, one that will lead you to that Innercosmic Highway that runs far above the limitations of the physical world.

Parts I, II, and III were originally three small books published by The Quartus Foundation—*Prayer, Principles & Power, The Manifestation Process,* and *Mastering Money.* The decision to edit, rewrite, and expand them based on new understanding, and consolidate the books into one volume, was made when I realized that the material in each was like a piece of a puzzle—and when brought together in sequence there would be greater clarity and continuity in solving the mystery of achieving dominion over "this world." In unity they would reveal the necessity of a firm foundation built on the Truth of Being (Part I), a method to duplicate the synchronous activity of Superconsciousness in fulfilling the needs experienced in the phenomenal world (Part II), and a deeper understanding of the principles involved in the materialization of form out of energy (Part III).

As we come into proper alignment with the awesome Power within, our Higher Nature, we are carried above the laws of the third-dimensional plane. We become a channel for the dynamic radiation of Will, Love, and Creative Intelligence that is tenaciously seeking an outlet through consciousness to reveal the New Reality of Heaven on Earth. But the personality must surrender the little i—that symbol of dualism with its separated head and body—so that the Master *I* may express in all Its power and glory. The goal of every student of Wisdom is to transform individual identity from the self who can do nothing to the Self Who is doing everything *now*. Once that shift takes place, the old life of emptiness, illness, and lack is transformed into a new state of *being* that experiences only fulfillment, wholeness, and abundance.

This is a book that should be studied, understood, and put into practice if the maximum benefit is to be realized. With that in mind, do not be in such a hurry to rush through each chapter. Take time to read, ponder, contemplate and meditate on the ideas presented. Work with the suggested programs and keep a spiritual diary of the changes taking place in your world—plus the new revelations and truths that will come forth from within.

You are a spiritual being embodying all of the Power of the Universe within you. Will you not accept this Truth and start living as the Light of the world that you are? The Dawn is approaching. . .it is time to awaken to your Inheritance.

John Randolph Price

PART I

Moving From an Attitude of Becoming to a Consciousness of Being

CHAPTER ONE

The Art and Science of Prayer

"Have you tried praying about the problem?"

If you have ever been asked that question you may have felt a twinge of anger or futility, because for many people in this world praying is totally meaningless, or is considered a roll of the dice while hoping for the best. The latter perspective places prayer in the category of a speculative venture—a gamble with the winds of fate. But even in games of chance a level of skill can be developed, and with prayer this is usually thought of as a different way of making contact with God and influencing the Supreme Being to perform a special miracle on our behalf—or for some metaphysicians, a new method to direct universal laws for personal gain.

At one time or another we all have discovered what we thought was the secret of successful prayer—*That's it!*—only to find that the next bended knee address to the Lord didn't get through—or the application of our tried and true transcendental formula came up empty. Believing that the heavenly lines were busy or that we dialed amiss, we tried again to reach the Higher Power and get our problems solved. And occasionally the Divine 911 number worked; at other times it appeared that we were put on hold while another call was accepted.

This whole idea of prayer is such a confusing subject that even Webster has difficulty in stating its meaning. *Pray* is defined as "to beg for imploringly"—and *prayer* is "the act or practice of praying, as to God"—i.e. asking the Creator for alms, being a beggar. No wonder God doesn't believe in call-forwarding. One of these days the collective mind of humanity, which is a part of each personal consciousness, will wake up to the fact that *prayer is nothing more than coming into alignment with the Higher Nature of individual being to release into expression that which already is.*

On a television show one evening, actress Joan Collins said, "I want it all and I want it now." Great! At least that's a starting point in realizing that we *already* have it all, and we have it *now.* You will see as you progress through this book that this isn't idle speculation. As individualizations of God, nothing was left out of our creation, which means that on the inner planes we already have everything that we could possibly desire. Accordingly, our prayer work should be to condition consciousness to serve as the outlet for all that we are and have to flow into perfect expression— and we do this through a higher degree of realization of Who and What we are, and through a deeper understanding of the finished Kingdom that was given to us in the beginning.

We look within and become consciously aware of the Master Self, our Great Superconsciousness with Its magnificent Domain of Completion, and we see that every need, desire, hope, and aspiration has already been fulfilled. And with power and authority we say I AM *THAT* I AM! We identify ourselves as Beings of God and we recognize that every aspect of the Kingdom is ours—that our cup eternally overflows with every good thing including abundance, beauty, creative expression, freedom, harmony, health, joy, love, peace, and right relations. And then we let our heightened awareness—our *consciousness*— interpret itself as that which we are conscious of being and having.

Simple? Yes, but not easy because we are bombarded with race mind thoughts that say we are less than Divine, and as inferior beings we must continually bargain and negotiate with God. Even when we discovered that the Presence was *within*, we sometimes felt that if we were persistent and forceful enough, we could squeeze the Power out into the phenomenal world to zap a problem for us. Since the art of prayer and the science of praying seem so complex, let's proceed now to gain a better understanding of this "approach to deity." We will begin by going back to about 500 B.C. and visit the Crotona Mystery School in Southern Italy, founded by Pythagoras, considered the first and greatest philosopher.

Pythagoras said that God, or Supreme Mind, was the Cause of all things, and since God was All Truth, then the effect of this Cause must be Truth, or Spiritual Reality—*when the individual was in harmony with Cause.* He believed that man need not ask for anything because the Intelligent Power of God was eternally providing all things necessary. Thus, the "secret" of prayer was to be in tune with Infinite Mind, which he said could be done through an understanding of the principles of three sciences: geometry, music, and astronomy.

When we look at the meaning behind these disciplines we can see the thrust of his teachings. Geometry: *the rules of logic and assumptions that we accept without proof.* Music: *vibrations, tones, and celestial harmonies.* Astronomy: *the order and elements of the universe.* Through these sciences the student learned to "live in the Cosmic Flow" by gaining a greater awareness of his/her relationship to the Higher Power, the Oneness of Life, and the loving givingness of God.

Today we also find many philosophers and mystics stressing the importance of "living by Grace"—of being an open channel through which Divine Consciousness fulfills itself. While Pythagoras' scientific training may not be necessary, a disciplining of the mind through meditation is emphasized, and the act of prayer is viewed as moving into a higher vibration to be of one accord with the Inner Presence—with all things "added" to the person's life and affairs.

Venturing back in time once again let's drop in on a Mystery School in Egypt and look at prayer from the Hermetic tradition. Here we notice that prayer is in the form of invocation-evocation, with special attention given to creative visualization. This is a structured form of prayer involving the radiation of power (invocation), the magnetic response through the law of attraction (evocation), with intensity and clarity of concentration (visualization) as the bridge between the two. The principle involved here is "To give is to receive; to receive is to give, and the circle becomes complete." The "giving" is radiation; "receiving" is attraction. Another way of looking at this principle is to understand that in invocation-evocation we are decreeing and drawing forth into our awareness *that which already is*. It is not creating something with the human mind that did not previously exist.

In modern language we would say that the framework of this form of prayer includes (1) a feeling of oneness with the Presence within, (2) a well-defined intention relating to the fulfillment of an unselfish desire—translated into a thought-form picturing the finished expression, (3) an intense radiation of the spiritual energy of the thought-form, using the power of will to extend the energy into the phenomenal world, (4) visualizing with great clarity the union of spirit and matter and the materialization of the thought-form, (5) arousing the feeling of magnetism in consciousness and seeing the finished form and experience being drawn into the individual's life, and (6) enjoying the new reality with great joy and thanksgiving through creative imagination.

Understand that this was not a mind over matter process, and neither did it involve the use of black/white magic to manipulate effects in the third-dimensional world. Rather, it was a system to lift consciousness above the individual's needs and problems and to clear the mind to behold the natural-order activity of the Divine Self. The intention simply brought one into accord with God's will; the radiation of the spiritual energy was to move the individual into harmony with the eternal givingness of the shining Self; the visualization was to see with the vision of Self; and the feeling of magnetism was an exercise in learning how to receive and accept the divine effects. As the mind is healed of the false belief that peace and joy in the phenomenal world are dependent on it to make something happen, the mind opens to the already-flowing energy moving into perfect manifestation. This radiation-magnetism approach, with some variations, continues to be used by many esoteric groups today.

As the Christian Church developed and canons and rituals were established, the method of prayer was condensed into five conditions, all based on scripture.

1. *Repentance*—"If my people who are called by my name humble themselves, and pray and seek my face, and turn from wicked ways, then I will hear from heaven, and will forgive their sin and heal their land." (2 Chronicles 7:14)

2. *Spiritual Desire*—"Ask and it will be given you. . ." (Luke 11:5-10)

3. *Sufficient trust in God to ask in prayer*—"You do not have because you do not ask." (James 4:2)

4. *Faith that God answers prayers*—"And whatever you ask in prayer, you will receive, if you have faith." (Matthew 21:22)

5. *Acceptance of the answered prayer*—"whatever you ask in prayer, believe that you have received it, and it will be yours." (Mark 11:24)

Conspicuous by its absence is the activity of controlled visualization, or seeing from the Highest Vision. It had been written, "Where there is no vision, the people perish." (Proverbs 29:18) And the Lord God had given the instruction to "Write the vision" in Habakkuk 2:2, but a passage in Genesis 6:5 raised the red flag: "The Lord saw that the wickedness of man was great in the earth, and that every imagination of the thoughts of his heart was only evil continually." This refers to the original descent of consciousness into the lower energies and the misuse of the imaging power by the personality.

Without the vision and an understanding of spiritual law, answered prayer was dependent on blind faith, and the petitioner was often referred to James 1:6-8 when prayers seemed to come up empty: "...let him ask in faith, with no doubting, for he who doubts is like a wave of the sea that is driven and tossed by the wind. For that person must not suppose that a double-minded man, unstable in all his ways, will receive anything from the Lord."

This "doubting" business was playing havoc with organized religion, so the church fathers came up with an answer: "Just relax and leave the praying to us; we will make contact with God for you." The idea of praying for others is certainly commendable, just as sharing the fruit of your garden would be, but the next step should have been to teach the masses the art and science of dynamic prayer—to demonstrate to others how to grow their own garden.

As the esoterists began to emerge again in the 16th century, the spiritual science of mind, energy, and manifestation gained a new foothold and humankind came out of the Dark Ages. In core groups throughout the world emphasis was once again placed on revealing the perfection of the individual through a consciousness of cosmic rhythm, universal order, and celestial harmony. The concept of productive prayer using creative visualization was also taught again. The doors to the new age of Enlightenment were slowly opening.

When Ralph Waldo Emerson and the Transcendentalists made waves in the 1800s, the strong currents of Self-reliance began to be felt in humanity's consciousness. Transcendentalism was the assertion that each individual has an intuitive capacity for grasping ultimate truth, and thus achieving a sure knowledge of a supernatural order beyond the reach of the senses. Emerson believed that God could be found in the depths of his own heart, and that with attentive ear he could hear the voice of God. Prayer, to Emerson, was "the contemplation of the facts of life from the highest point of view. It is the soliloquy of a beholding and jubilant soul. It is the spirit of God pronouncing his works good."

Within a few years the new Thought Movement was underway with the founding of Unity (Charles and Myrtle

Fillmore), Divine Science (Nona Books), and Religious Science (Ernest Holmes). In the *Metaphysical Bible Dictionary*[1] containing Charles Fillmore's teachings, we find prayer described in this manner: "In true prayer we take with us words of Truth, a statement of Truth, or an affirmation, and turn our attention within to the very center of our being, where the Father dwells. We affirm these words of Truth and meditate on them, then get very still and wait in the silence for God to make them real to us."

Regarding the use of imagination, Fillmore writes in *The Twelve Powers of Man*[2]—"It is through the imagination that the formless takes form. Man and the universe are a series of pictures in the Mind of Being. God made man in His image and likeness. Man, in his turn, is continually making and sending forth into his mind, his body, and the world about him living thought forms embodied and indued with his whole character."

From Ernest Holmes' writings in *The Science of Mind*[3] we read: "There is a place in us which lies open to the infinite; but when the spirit brings Its gift, by pouring Itself through us, It can give to us only what we take. This taking is mental. If we persist in saying that Life will not give us that which is good (God will not answer my prayer) It cannot, for Life must reveal Itself to us through our Intelligence. The pent-up energy of Life, and the possibility of further human evolution, works through man's imagination and will."

Decide on your method of prayer and give it a chance to work. More prayers are aborted on the day they were to become visible in form and experience than we can possibly imagine. The reason: the individual "saw" the prayer unanswered and felt that the good would not come to pass, thus destroying the emerging thought-form and silencing the Word that was even then being made flesh.

How should you pray? That depends on where you are in consciousness, and there are many techniques and formulas to work with to align yourself with your Higher Nature to release the All-Good into expression. Included is the practice of keeping your mind stayed on the Presence within and being a beholder of the activity of God taking place through you. There is the invocation (radiation)-evocation (attraction) technique outlined previously, the manifestation process discussed in Part II of this book, and the consciousness-expansion activities detailed in Part III. Many students on the path also have periods of meditation on the Truth of their Being followed by visualization of the ideal conditions, and a complete releasing of the scenario to Spirit. Some people simply discuss their problems with God, ask for a divine solution, and go on their way with faith in the outcome. Others begin each day forgiving everyone including themselves and surrendering everything to God, thus lifting consciousness above the seeming problems where they are solved by the Higher Power.

Personally, my spiritual work is based on the tone and pitch of my consciousness on any particular day. Sometimes I take a few seed thoughts of Truth into meditation, let them expand, and then listen to the voice within reveal the external realities. This moves consciousness into a higher vibration to function as a more suitable inlet and outlet for the action of Self. Frequently I will meditate on the Presence within as the Source and Substance of that which appears to be lacking in the phenomenal world—to change the frequency of my consciousness to be of one accord with the Master Self. (My consciousness of God *as* my supply *is* my supply.) And when my mind seems so fractured that I am totally out of focus, I'll sit in my chair and love my Holy Self with all the feeling I have and feel the love returning, continuing until the cobwebs have cleared.

On other occasions I will work with the creative energies in the radiation-attraction process to simulate the divine activity. Again, the objective is not to influence the Master Self or create something on my own. It is to heal my mind of any false beliefs that the miracle-working Power of God has somehow been shut down. We should never forget that our Divine Self always knows our needs and is constantly meeting every challenge, but this healing-correcting energy can only flow through a consciousness that *knows* this Truth. So effective prayer is really the art and science of healing our own personal minds so that we may be a fit channel for Spirit.

One of my favorite forms of healing prayer is what I call the "Spiritual Identity" meditation, and its seed was found in Emerson's writings: "The simplest person who in his integrity worships God becomes God." This meditative prayer is based on the Fact that my real name (and yours) is. . .*I*. That is the name one uses when referring to personal individuality. It is also the secret word used throughout the Bible and other sacred literature to designate the individualized Presence of God, which is your true Identity. (We're not adding the **AM** to the *I* yet; that comes later as a way of anchoring spirituality in the Earth plane.) So your proper name is none other than *I*. That *I* is the Truth of you, the Self of you, the Spirit and Soul of you. It is God being you!

Every problem that any of us could possibly have on Earth is because of an identification with our personality and not our Individuality. Accordingly, when we identify ourselves with Reality and hold to that awareness, our consciousness of the Divine Self becomes as one—as two sides of a window pane with nothing in between to block the light.

Let us take this understanding a step further. We know that the Spirit of God cannot suffer lack, limitation, illness, or strained/broken relationships. We know that Spirit, which includes All, could never be without anything. And we know that this indwelling Master Self is never unemployed, underemployed, unfulfilled, confused, fearful, resentful, or any other characteristic attributed to the lower nature of humanhood. This Holy *I is* all, *knows* all, *does* all—and it is only when the little "i" gets in the way that we block the being, the knowing, and the doing. But you are not the "i." The "i" is a human creation formulated through ignorance—a mutation that exists only through false beliefs and sustained only by the power of error thinking, yet it can be redeemed by the acceptance of the *I*.

When you think, speak, or write *I*, you are not (or should not) be referring to the you who has no wisdom, no power, no vision. You are (or should be) thinking of the Master Self within—that Spirit of God as you Who is the I-Omniscient, the I-Omnipotent. So the first step in training for this particular method of prayer is to meditate, contemplate, ponder on *I* as the God-Self within. Look again at these Bible passages from the perspective of *I.*

> The *I* is my shepherd; I shall not want.
> The *I* is my light and my salvation; whom shall I fear?
> As long as he sought the *I,* God made him to prosper.
> Be still, and know that *I* am God.
> *I* who speaks am he.
> *I* am the bread of life.
> *I* said, you are gods.
> *I* am the resurrection and the life.
> *I* have come as light into the world.
> *I* am the way, the truth, and the life.
> My peace *I* give to you.

Understand that the objective of this way of thinking and praying is not to destroy or eliminate the personality. Rather, it is to move the lower nature into its rightful position as a witness to the Divine Activity of the *I.* We want to get to the point where the little self says, "I realize that as a human being I don't have all the answers, nor do I have the power to change my life from lack to abundance, from illness to wholeness, from discord to harmony. In fact, all the praying by humans over thousands of years has done very little for this planet and conditions in the world. So maybe it's about time to get my humanity out of the way and let my divinity take over. Of course, I understand that I have my part to play in this dramatic comedy called life, but I'm up to it and I really get excited when I consider that my world will be a reflection of God instead of my ego. My role in the scheme of things is to simply be aware, to recognize, to be conscious of the activity of the *I* within— the activities of true place, abundance, wholeness, right relations, safety and protection, fulfillment, love, and joy. The list of good things and experiences is endless, and all that I have to do is keep my mind focused on the Master Self within and I am kept in perfect peace."

When you transfer the thrust of your living from the little "i" to the Supreme *I,* you are also taking the burden off your shoulders and giving it to the Omnipotent Self who eliminates burdens in the twinkling of an eye. You are handing over the reins of government—the governing of your world—to the *Master I* who not only knows how to superbly administer, manage, guide, and oversee all of your affairs, but is willing to take over and do it now! After all, it's the *I*'s life we are talking about—the *I*'s body, bank account, and relationships—so don't you think that the rightful *I* should be in charge?

As your mind and emotions begin to grasp the Truth of the *I*, you will begin to understand that you do not have any problems, that you do not need anything, that there is nothing to heal or fix or manipulate or possess. Everything just *is* right now—*is* harmonious, whole, and complete. Why? Because *I* is!

The meditative prayer in four parts. First, look within and contemplate that Magnificent *I* that you are in Truth and begin the releasing process. Release your body, bank account, debts, relationships, job, fears, unforgiveness, uncertainties, confusion—and your past, present, and future. Surrender all to the Self who has wanted to move back into the driver's seat since the moment the ego took control. That is the beginning phase of this method of prayer.

The second step is to let the *Master I* be in Earth as It is in Heaven, and you do this by adding the word **AM**. Work on this exercise for a few moments: Say to yourself silently, "I AM." Then imagine that you are hearing the Master Self within speaking the same words, *"I AM"*. Usually the words as registered in the mind and feeling nature will seem to come from two different coordinates in consciousness, so your objective is to align the two **I AM**s into one voice. Keep repeating the process, silently speaking "I AM" and listening with the inner ear to Self saying *"I AM"*—and each time feel the two voices drawing closer and closer together until there is only one *I AM*.

Once you do this you are ready for the third step, the Identity Prayer. Meditate slowly on these ideas, pausing to contemplate each line with great feeling:

The I AM Self in the midst of me is Omnipotent, All Knowing, All Seeing, eternally Doing and Being.

I know this. I feel this. I am aware of the radiating Energy of the I AM Self going before me, creating according to the Perfect Patterns, revealing the Divine Standard of wholeness, abundance, right relations, and true place fulfillment.

Pause and feel the radiation of Divine Energy from your entire being. After a few moments continue the meditation.

I AM shining abundance. I AM wholeness flowing into perfect expression. I AM the radiation of unconditional love. I AM the light of harmony, the beam of happiness, the ray of contentment. I AM all. ALL that I could ever see, I AM. Because I AM all, I HAVE all. Through the eyes of the I AM Self I now see the High Vision of completeness, divine order, and glorious harmony in the world. The Divine Have is in perfect expression.

Pause again for a few moments and see in your mind's eye—with controlled visualization—everything as perfect in your life. Feel with your emotions what you are seeing: a Life Experience of total joy, love, beauty, abundance, wholeness, harmony, creativity, an easy flow of accomplishment, great peace and contentment. Keep watching the *controlled* mental movie until you are completely satisfied that every activity in your life is in divine order—then expand your vision to see people throughout the world enjoying a Life Experience as fulfilling as yours. Then return to the meditation.

I have seen the Truth. My affairs are now an extension of the I AM Self, an expression of my Divine Consciousness. Because I HAVE all, there is nothing more to seek. I now live as the I THAT I AM. I have moved from an attitude of becoming to a Consciousness of Being. I now rest in my Beingness.

Be still and rest now in the Presence of your Holy Self, listening to the inner Voice.

From the moment the meditation is concluded you move into the fourth step, which is to live your life as a prayer.

To look into someone's eyes and behold the *I* is a prayer. To silently communicate with Nature, recognizing the *I* in all, is a prayer. To forgive all is a prayer. Gratitude is a prayer. Sharing is a prayer. Everything you do should be a prayer—and continuously flowing through your mind are the words, "The *I* is doing and being everything now; I cannot want for anything!" You live the prayer and the prayer lives you, and taking thought for tomorrow is replaced by living in the joyful now.

CHAPTER TWO

Blessing All and Praying for Others

Late one evening on the hillside where we lived, I was so filled with the love for Earth, her people, and all forms of life that I suddenly exclaimed in a loud voice, "God bless this world!" And then I thought about what I had said, wondering about the audacity of directing the Source from Whom all blessings flow to do something that was *already* being done. If one believes in an eternally loving and constantly giving Omnipresence, and I do, then what does it mean to "bless" a person or a planet?

As I was contemplating these thoughts I experienced a "flow-through" that said, "The act of blessing another is to offer yourself as a channel for the activity of Spirit. When you bless an individual, a form, or a situation, you become the instrument through which divine energy flows to adjust, heal, and elevate consciousness."

Think about that. To bless is to connect the radiation of Self (the *I*) and the object of the blessing in a focused cord of light. Jesus came into this world to bless it, offering himself as a Divine Channel for Supreme Being. That is our role, too—even before we reach his level of consciousness. We begin where we are to do our part in reconnecting the third and fourth dimensions—to be a conduit between Earth and Heaven for the dynamic Will of God.

Webster says that *bless* means "to invoke divine care for; to praise; glorify; to confer prosperity or happiness upon; to protect, preserve." The Tibetan Master, Djwhal Khul, says: "From the place wherein your physical plane life is lived, let there go forth that which can heal and bless. Nothing can stop this blessing; it speeds forth upon the wings of detachment and from a heart that has no care for itself. . ."[1] And the Bible is full of "bless" and "blessing" references, but seldom do we pause to consider that each one of us has the awesome power to bless another and melt away the third dimensional illusion. We *do* have the Divine Authority to invoke divine care, praise, glorify, confer prosperity, protect, and preserve—if we choose to be the instrument for the power.

In this context, to bless someone or something is so much more than muttering words of endearment or finding another way of expressing gratitude. In truth, it is taking an action in consciousness with words to lift the recipient of the blessing back up to the Divine Standard of Harmony. So the next time you utter a blessing, think about what you are doing. Focus the mind to channel the energy, open your heart to make the connection with the object of the blessing, and speak the words to release the power.

There is no manipulation involved, no attempt to influence or interfere with free will, so you need not wait until you are asked for assistance to give your blessings. Just bless everyone and everything, including yourself. Take time each day to bless your body, bank account, home, car, family, friends, your work and place of employment, your nation, *all* nations and their leaders, and all of the kingdoms—mineral, plant, animal, and human. And when you hear someone blessing you, just remember that you are being touched by the Light and Love of *I*—the Omnipotent Spirit of God—through the person conferring the blessing.

Praying for Others

In the previous chapter we talked about prayer as the activity of coming into alignment with the *I* in order to release into expression that which already is—with the emphasis for the most part on praying for one's self. Now let's talk about praying for others, as an extension to the act of blessing.

When you have evolved in consciousness to the point where the *I* is realized, one requiring assistance simply says to you, "I need your prayers." A connection in consciousness will have been made and the one seeking help receives the healing without effort on your part. Remember, it is the Master within Who heals. Until we have the Realization Experience, however, we work from where we are—regardless how faint our awareness of the God Presence may be. Just know that even if a flicker of the healing light gets through a crack in our opaqueness, a positive benefit will occur. And the more transparent we are, the greater the results. Sometimes the effects are immediate; at other times the harmonizing of the situation is gradual—but in retrospect it is seen as the logical working out of a problem according to cosmic law.

Here is one example of a highly effective method that may be used if someone asks for your prayers. Go into a meditative state to realize as clearly as possible the reality and perfection of your own Inner Self. Contemplate with "relaxed intensity" the attributes of the Infinite *I*, the God-Self that you are. Ponder the incredible Love, the infinite Wisdom, the perfect Life, the radiant Light, the dynamic Will, the awesome Power, the absolute Truth. As the feeling of the Presence begins to expand in your consciousness, pour all the love of your being into that Presence. Let love fill you and wash over you and spill out before you until love is the dominant vibration of your entire consciousness. At that point gently bring the individual who has asked for your prayers into your awareness. See the individual clearly, or if you do not know the individual personally, simply see his or her name in a circle of light. Now begin to flood that person (or the name in the circle) with your love. See the love flowing from you in streams of radiant energy, literally saturating and enveloping the person or circle. Keep radiating the love and watching the scene in your mind until the object is seen only as a brilliant energy field of Love-Light. Now slowly withdraw your attention, as if moving away from the object, and consciously release the person to Spirit. The more you practice this technique the more proficient you will become.

Another method that has produced seeming miracles is almost like the above process in reverse. You begin with the person's name or face/form etched firmly in your mind, and lovingly contemplate the individual. After a moment or two begin to meditate on *your* Truth of Being, your Holy Self, and keep at it until the person or name completely disappears from consciousness and your entire focus is on the Presence within. Even if you can only "forget" the individual for a few seconds while your mind is totally on God, the results will be amazing. The reason: the individual moved out of your human consciousness into the pure Essence of Spirit where no disease or lack exists.

One particular healing group I know of uses a process they call "window cleaning." They work on the inner planes to affect a cleansing of the person's energy field and alter the vibrational pitch, thus removing the blocks that may have unconsciously been imposed. When the individual is clear of these pockets of misqualified energy, the Spiritual Self shines through in all its glory to straighten out the crooked places and make all things new. Understand that praying for others or altering vibrations is not performing magic, and neither is it giving someone a "fix" (you are a metaphysician, not a meta-fixer). This absent healing work is simply cooperating with Spirit for the benefit of another.

Sometimes an overt action—a reaching out for help—is all that is needed to change the vibration in consciousness and release the healing currents. One day a woman wrote me about her son, explaining the serious situation he was in and asking for our prayers. Well, the letter was lost in the mail and I did not receive it until two weeks after the postmark date—the same day that the woman called me to express her gratitude for the "miracle" involving her son. She said that within a few days after she wrote the letter "everything came up roses." When I told her that we had just received the letter that very morning she was shocked, but I went on to explain that she had obviously released her fear and anxiety by writing the letter. When she became centered in a higher *faith* vibration, her consciousness served as an outlet for Spirit to do its mighty work.

Our ongoing research at The Quartus Foundation tells us that the results of prayers and spiritual treatments on behalf of others may only be temporary, that unless the consciousness that produced the problem in the first place is changed, the negative situation may reoccur. This is why I so strongly emphasize to others the vital importance of daily spiritual study, prayer and meditation, listening to the inner Voice, journal writing, thought management, emotional control, harmlessness in actions, communing with Nature, and living the highest Truth. We all came back into physical form to awaken to our true Identity and move above the woes and sorrows of the third dimension, and we must not let anything stand in the way of fulfilling that mission and purpose. At the same time, we must never forget another reason that we are here on Planet Earth. We are here to be of service to humanity and to do all that we can to assist our brothers and sisters awaken from the dream state. And if that requires a healing in mind, body, pocketbook, or relationships, let's do it with love and joy, and with gratitude for the opportunity to serve.

I realize that some people hesitate for one reason or another to ask for help. One young man told me that he did not reach out for assistance because he wanted to heal himself. That's fine, unless it is ego talking. Healing *is* a do-it-yourself project when we have the consciousness for it. In fact, we are to become so transparent to Spirit that challenges are caught and dissolved before they even reach us. But until we reach this illumined state, let's ask for help when we need it. Just know that requesting assistance with challenges does not make you appear less spiritual.

If you feel trapped in the darkness, reach out to the person or group where you feel an affinity and ask for support. You don't have to discuss your situation or even say what the nature of the problem is. Just say—"I need your help"—and a spiritual friend will be glad to walk through the tunnel with you in Consciousness, into the Light at the other end.

CHAPTER THREE

Understanding
Spiritual Principles

Playing golf was one of those business-related activities that I gave up when I left the corporate world, and neither decision left me with any regrets.

Never having taken any formal lessons, I learned to play the game through experience and the helpful hints of others. It had seemed so easy when I first walked the course with a good friend. Just hit the little white ball and get it into the hole in less strokes than it takes your opponent. My first nine holes proved me wrong. I was constantly in the woods, water, and sand—and I thought this was supposed to be fun. Next time, in a foursome, my partner tried to help. "Keep your head down. . .eye on the ball. . .correct your grip. . .widen your stance. . .left arm in. . .slow your backswing. . .follow through"—and on and on.

Until the process became automatic (the principles of the game realized), the whole operation was a trial and error mechanical approach, all dependent on thinking out every step, remembering all the little nuances, and being totally aware of the action to be taken at each precise moment.

While it may be stretching a point, living the spiritual life is much like playing golf. There are certain principles involved, and until those principles are fully mastered, we have not entered into a consciousness of mastery. Webster defines *principle* as "a fundamental law, primary source, origin"—terms that we often refer to when thinking about God. But just thinking about golf will not turn us into a pro, and neither will thinking of things spiritual make us a master. We must learn the fundamentals of the law and know the principles involved in the Mind of Pure Being and Its expressions from the formless into the formed. Since we as individuals are an integral part of this Manifestation Chain, we are not going to live a whole, abundant, fulfilling, joyous, and free life unless we can pin-point exactly who and what we are and understand our part in the process. As the old saying goes, "Ignorance of the law is no excuse."

To be able to truly live in the present moment, let us return to the beginning with a renewed understanding of. . .

GOD. The Infinite *IS*, Eternal Existence, the Sum-Total of all Masculine and Feminine Energies; the Formless One; Omnipresent, Omnipotent, Omniscient.

SON. The Supreme Being's Image of Itself in Infinite Mind appearing as the Omnipresent Spirit of God; an altering of the Divine Vibration in the Cosmic Energy Field to behold the male-female Principle of the "one Son"—the Divine Selfhood. To continue creation, the Universal Spirit of the Divine Selfhood expressed Itself as an infinite number of Individual Beings, as the sun extends its rays. (*Individual*: "not divisible, not separable"—Webster.) We are the male-female God-Sun in individual expression, God's Omnipresent Spirit-Self particularized as perfect Beings of Light—with all that God is as our Essential Nature.

HOLY SPIRIT. The "Light of the Sun"—the Radiance of Truth shining from the Divine Individuality into personal consciousness—the Energy of Divine Intelligence and the Fire of Divine Inspiration that will correct the false beliefs and error patterns in mind when accepted by the personality.

MIND. The Creative Factor extending from Universal Being through Individual Being and reflected in the personality. This is the only Mind we have; it is the only Mind there is.

CONSCIOUSNESS. The Divine Self sent forth a stream of Consciousness into the Earth plane; a beam of Mind was extended into the potential world of manifest form to be *aware* of terrestrial existence so that creation could continue on all planes. The Bible symbology of the Garden of Eden experience barely hints at this immense drama. Our Self imaged the Idea of Itself in the world of matter, and out of Its Energy (dust) appeared Its Expression. The "breath of life" referred to in Genesis 2:7 is the *stream of Consciousness* extended downward. (The root of "breath" is *stream.*) But Mind cannot separate from Mind—therefore, within the stream of Consciousness was the Mind of Divine Self, later referred to as "the indwelling Presence," "Christ in you,"and "the Kingdom of God within."

The Nature of Divine Self is such that It cannot be directly involved with effects. Reason: that which is eternal and infinite cannot change Its Nature and become temporary and finite. Therefore, Consciousness, later called "the Son of Man," was lowered in vibration to function as a channel for the outpouring of Divine Self. Out of the undifferentiated Consciousness of Self a Stream of Awareness was extended to distinguish the creations—the naming of the effects in Gen. 2:19. Since there was no separation from the Mind of Self, Consciousness continued to have the will-power of Self, yet its function was to be *aware* of its Identity and be a witness to the Divine Activity of Creation taking place through it.

In the beginning on the Earth plane, Consciousness was composed of a Light Body; a Mental Body of spiritual awareness, understanding, and knowledge; and an outer shell of cosmic etheric matter. (All forms, animate and inanimate, were etheric and not concretized.) In time, and to assist in the acceleration of the creative process, Divine Self extended the feminine aspect of Being into Consciousness. The "rib" reference in Genesis can be traced to the root word of *crown,* thus Consciousness was "crowned" (fulfilled) with the investment of the feeling nature.

Over a period of millions of years Consciousness began to feel an affection for the experience of external expression, a feeling symbolized by the serpent in Genesis. Consciousness was beginning to identify Itself with the effects of the world—and the etheric body, with its lines of force and light, was energized and a physical body slowly formed. When the physical eyes were finally opened (Gen. 3:7), Consciousness saw that it was imprisoned in form and felt *naked*—"without protection or defense" (Webster). And what we now call "personality" came into existence.

PERSONALITY. In its higher state it is personal consciousness awakening to the Truth of Divine Reality; in the lower it is the mask worn by consciousness symbolizing an image of itself as other than its Divine Origin—the descent of conscious knowing into judgement and the formation of beliefs. And through the judging of appearances, error thoughts emerged on the screen of mind and false beliefs were accepted.

EGO. Written with lower case "e" the ego represents the sum-total of all error thoughts and false beliefs concentrated in a self-created thought-form hovering in consciousness. It is totally identified with the physical body and all other outer effects.

PHYSICAL BODY. A vehicle for identification in form and for relating to other personalities. The body is the material aspect of the auric egg and is surrounded by the etheric, emotional, mental, and cosmic energies in a Force Field. It has no mind of its own and simply reflects consciousness. It is also the symbol of the separation because an individual who totally identifies with a physical body cannot see him/her self as an incorporeal Being of Light, a direct extension of the Light of God.

GUILT. The result of actions taken in thought, word, and deed by the personality; self-reproach based on the belief that one has done something wrong, resulting in a sense of incompleteness, insecurity, inferiority, and unfulfillment—all feelings of guilt. The human ancestral code in the collective consciousness says that such feelings emanating from the commitment of offenses must be punished.

FEAR. Anxiety, dread—to be afraid of the punishment. The energy of fear *attracts*, therefore we punish ourselves by the conclusion reached in mind that the punishment is justified. Thus, a *decision for fear* is made. The root of fear is the belief that personal consciousness is more powerful than God, otherwise the maladies of humankind would not exist. Because we are seemingly separated from God, *we* must have caused hell on earth to appear, and we believe that we must suffer the consequences of this demonstration of omnipotence. Therefore, we have chosen to be weak to restore power to God, and we chose scarcity, sickness, sadness, and suffering as our way, truth, and life.

THE PRONOUNCEMENT OF INNOCENCE. Genesis is symbolic, an allegory written and rewritten with translations of translations passed down through time. Taken literally it in no way parallels the creation story as taught in the Sacred Academies of the ancient past, nor does it relate to the beginning of the races as revealed by the Sages and Masters throughout recorded history. Individual Being has never sinned, and Its extended Consciousness was certainly not cursed by God and banished from heaven with multiplied pain and servitude for women, and endless toil and suffering for men. The truth is, we simply descended into matter for the joy of continuing creation, found that terrestrial existence can be illusory, identified with the illusion, temporarily lost our awareness of our Divine Identity, and began the evolutionary journey back into full spiritual consciousness. No crime committed, no reason for an eternal guilt trip, and no need for punishment. And one of these days the race consciousness will understand this and "Streaks of lightning will flash from one end of the world to the other, growing ever brighter until the era of darkness is brought utterly to an end." (From the Dead Sea Scrolls[1])

With this overview as our basis, let's proceed now to define twelve specific principles:

1. **God Is.**

2. **The Highest Aspect of Individual Being is the Pure Spirit of God, the Omnipresent Selfhood embodying the fullness of the Godhead.** This Universal Sonship extends Itself as. . .

3. **The Second Aspect of Individual Being, the particularized Higher or Master Self—also known as the Christ Self, Son of God, Soul (cap. S), Superconsciousness, the Holy *I*.** The Master Self reflects Itself as. . .

4. **The Third Aspect of Individual Being, Spiritual Consciousness.** This Aspect has been called the Awakening Mind of Personality—the "Integrated Personality" where the mask of the not-self has been removed. It is the awareness within the man or woman of the Holy Reality within. Below this level is the sleeping "human"—the lower nature that continues to use the one Mind in its creative dream state under the dominance of ego. With each degree of realized Truth, the ego's control is lessened and the Higher Nature expands in the lower. The Holy Spirit is the Shining Link between Self and personality, serving as the Voice of Guidance and the Energy of Correction to heal the sense of separation and fully remove the mask of personal consciousness.

5. **When we know our Self, we know God.** This Self represents the creative power of God; It is the Center through which the God-Power flows. When contact is made with the Master Self, conscious contact with God is established, and this is why the admonition to KNOW THYSELF is one of the first lessons in life.

6. **The Supreme Being created us out of Itself, therefore we are perfect.** The Divine Imprint of God's Image of Itself on the Universal Substance can never be changed. The original Design of Being was pronounced flawless and must remain so throughout eternity.

7. **Consciousness always outpictures its dominant vibration; our world is a mirror of our convictions.** Universal Law says that a person's life and affairs are a reflection of his/her consciousness. Without the spiritual vibration of the Higher Self, the lower nature objectifies the dominant beliefs of the race mind and the personal ego, which includes a fascination with duality and opposites— good and evil, wholeness and illness, plenty and poverty.

8. **The Divine Consciousness of the Master Self expresses through a personality of a like vibration.** The Master Self sees, knows, and is only wholeness, fulfillment, abun-

dance, joy, peace, love, life, beauty, freedom, harmony, divine order, and perfection. This is the Truth of our Being, yet this Divine Consciousness can only manifest the fullness of Its Nature through a state of consciousness with a corresponding vibration.

9. **The lower nature must be redeemed if the Law is to be fulfilled.** The function of the lower nature (mind and emotions) is to be a proper channel through which the Higher Nature works. The role of the personality is to fulfill the Law of Correspondence—"as above, so below." It does this by coming into alignment with the Divine Self. This alignment is accomplished initially through meditation on the inner Presence. As the personality takes on more of the Divine Energy, it is taught harmlessness, unconditional love, gratitude, right relations, and world service—all of which help to deepen and expand the awareness of the Master One within.

10. **The more spiritual we are in our thoughts and feelings, the greater the harmony in our lives.** The phenomenal world is always a reflection of the physical plane consciousness; it is a mirror of that state of consciousness that is closest to it. Therefore, it behooves us to change our consciousness in order to create (reveal) a new model of Reality in the outer world. The more we are consciously aware of the Higher Self, the more the energy of that Presence fills our consciousness—and the greater the infilling of this energy, the greater the change for good in our third-dimensional world.

11. **Our consciousness of God AS that which we seek IS that which we seek.** The creative energy flows from the Divine Consciousness within through the lower nature. The attributes that are deemed to be the essential essence of the energy by the conscious mind are the ones more readily expressed on the physical plane. For example, a recognition of the wholeness and health as being the true nature of the radiating energy creates an awareness in mind that the *Source* of wellness is within. An identification of abundance as being the reality of this flowing energy registers in mind that the *Source* of abundance is indwelling. This consciousness of the Presence within as the

Source and Activity of health and abundance constitutes wholeness in body and an all-sufficiency of supply, which are then outpictured in visible form. Our consciousness OF God AS our (whatever) IS our (whatever).

12. **Continuous spiritual infilling results in the Realization Experience, leading in time to the fusion of personality and Self.** During the infilling process (receiving the radiating energy of the Master Self), the lower nature approaches a point where the higher energy begins to overshadow or outweigh the lower nature. This triggers a realization response and imparts a new level of understanding to the mind and emotions of the lower nature, which is reflected in the outer world as greater and greater degrees of harmony. Eventually the lower nature fades out and the Higher Self is in total control. Humanhood has been replaced with Divine Selfhood and the dynamic Will of God is made manifest in the physical plane of Earth as it is in the spiritual plane of Heaven.

Let's remember that each one of us is a complex creation composed of the Will and Power of God, the Love and Wisdom of Self, the Intelligence and Inspiration of Spirit, and the mind and emotions of personality. And we range from Pure Spirit all the way down (or out) to the dense physical body. From the Stillness of the Absolute to the intense vibratory activity of the phenomenal world, that holy channel must be reopened. The Rainbow Bridge must be rebuilt if we are to reexperience the Glory that we had in the beginning.

We cannot be effective creators and builders if we do not know ourselves literally from top to bottom, so let's begin now to comprehend our Wholeness intellectually, understand our Holiness emotionally, and let the Truth of our Being be realized spiritually.

A Contemplative Meditation

I was created as a Supreme Expression of Supreme Being. I did not create myself. God extended Itself and expressed Itself as the Individual Being I AM. Therefore, all that God is, I AM. I AM one whole Being—a thinking, knowing, understanding, loving, omnipotent Self endowed with the free gift of God's will to continue the creative process of all that which is good, true, and beautiful.

If my circle of life does not reflect this Truth of wholeness and harmony, it is because of an interlocking chain of beliefs, the sum-total of which form the self-created ego. The ego is the idea that I made up about myself; it is my image of myself. The energy of these ego beliefs blocks the natural flow of spiritual energy into matter, but I do not have to continue believing these beliefs. I can change my mind, and I choose to do so beginning now.

My mind is the agent of the Master Self within. It is an extension of the Light from on High, and therefore my mind is powerfully creative. Everything that is not perfect in my life is a manifestation of false beliefs in my mind, and all false beliefs are related to fear. What I am afraid of produces false beliefs. What am I afraid of? Regardless of my answer, it is the subconscious fear that I am more powerful than God.

My evidence of this is my body, my relationships, my financial affairs, and the overall condition of my life. God does not cause, will, or authorize sickness, discord, lack, or unfulfillment, yet I have experienced these things, which had led to the apprehension that I have the power to countermand the Divine Principles. I became afraid of my power, and therefore I chose to be weak to restore power to God. The root fear that I can override God's will has also resulted in a parent belief that says, "The world of effects with which I identify has more power than God." And the outcroppings of this belief have multiplied into a family of beliefs, such as:

1. My insufficiency is related to the country's economic condition.

2. My body can create sickness and disease.

3. The friction in my relationships is caused by other people.

4. My disappointments and failures are because of the economy, my employer, or other people in the workplace.

These are all false beliefs that have externalized in my world as more lack, more suffering, more discord, and more failures.

The first step out of this quagmire is to say to myself with passionate feeling: **"I choose not to believe falsely because**

43

there is nothing beneficial in such beliefs." I had chosen to believe these thoughts, therefore it was the thoughts in my mind that produced the disharmony and not the effects of my world, for effects are not cause. My insufficiency is not connected at all to any economic situation. My physical ailments are never related to my body. The problem in any relationship has nothing to do with another person. My disappointments and failures in my work are far removed from the economy, employer, or other people in the workplace. By understanding this and placing the responsibility where it belongs, I realize that no one has ever done anything to me. It was all the error thoughts in my mind being outpictured.

The second step out of this madness is to call in the cold Fire of Spirit to burn away all residue of my former system of false beliefs and error patterns. I do that now with deep passionate feeling.

Spirit of the Living Fire, pour Thyself on me that I may be consumed in the flames of purification. I cast all beliefs into the all-consuming fire; I let all error thoughts burn in the purifying fire; I let my judging emotions pass away in the loving fire; I find my freedom in the cleansing fire; I see myself healed in the invisible fire. I rest in the Living Fire, and I become the Spiritual Fire.

The third step in my escape from prison is to withdraw all resentment toward anyone or anything in the outer world. No one, no thing, has ever done anything to me, so I pull back all projections of ill will, hurt feelings, and irritation. This is what it means to forgive. And I forgive myself by withdrawing all displeasure with myself, knowing that under ego influence I simply made the mistake of believing in something that was not real. But I have changed my mind.

And the fourth step toward freedom is look up to Truth, to reconnect with the Light in consciousness and accept the radiation of Divine Love flowing from Above—and to think thoughts based only on the Principle of Truth. My commitment now is to use my mind as a channel for the Master Self I AM, as it was at the beginning of creation.

And the creation begins anew this day.

CHAPTER FOUR

More Pointers on Principles

As we have discussed, a principle is a law, and a law simply describes how something works. In the case of spiritual principles and laws, we are looking at an accumulated Body of Knowledge that has as its intention the healing of the sense of separation and the Divine Awakening of humanity. There are countless ways to explain the rules of mind and action (principles) relating to Truth, thus the frequent use of parables and analogies in spiritual teachings and esoteric literature. Accordingly, in the following "pointers" I have attempted to throw some new light on certain principles, which may help you avoid a few snares and traps on your journey.

Pointer No. 1: *Frozen Truth can make you numb.*
Many people who have studied Truth for decades may not have progressed any further than a few yards from the bottom of the mountain. One reason is that they have found a metaphysical comfort zone that feels most pleasant, and after a time the mind becomes numb, the vision tunneled, and the feeling nature concretized. This "don't confuse me with facts" syndrome can usually be spotted when an individual begins to be a bit dogmatic

regarding a particular teaching, referring to it as "the highest" or "the most authoritative" or "the last word." Personally I do not feel that such descriptions fit anything yet written on Planet Earth, and certainly no person on either side of the veil has yet communicated more than just a few fragments of what could be called the Final Truth.

Truth is infinite and absolute in the Mind of God, but each individual has access only to his/her *understanding* of Truth as it unfolds in consciousness. Thus, there is no *final* wisdom teaching. Even the Masters of the Hierarchy say that they are still evolving "into the Great Unknown."

My point? Do not limit the unfolding of your consciousness of Truth by focusing exclusively on a single teaching. Do not freeze your mind by refusing to at least entertain new ideas and concepts—even if at first they are beyond your present level of understanding. This does not mean that you are to agree with everything you read or hear. I certainly don't. For example, someone sent us a channeled book that did not resonate at all with my spiritual vibrations. While there are gems of wisdom coming down from higher realms, there is also some pure nonsense filtering in from the astral plane dressed in the clothing of spiritual communications, and we have to be careful that we are not snookered by sophistry.

We must practice discernment, which is a part of the spiritual learning process. But "nothing ventured nothing gained"—so let yourself be exposed to spiritual fact and fiction, always alert to your intuitive feelings about the *rightness* of the message. Someone's imagination disguised as revelations from on High could trigger an "I don't believe that" response, which may force you to closely examine what you *do* believe. And if you are writing daily in your spiritual journal, your Body of Truth will expand as you search your mind and heart for Divine Realities— the ones that are being formulated through *your* reasoning, *your* feelings, *your* interpretations of Truth.

As you broaden your horizons, do not be deceived into believing that you are going beyond the ideas that brought you where you are on the spiritual path. You cannot go *beyond* a basic and traditional Ancient Wisdom or New

Thought teaching; you can only move horizontally. You can proceed laterally along the line exploring a vast variety of teachings from Blavatsky, Bailey, Quimby, Fillmore, Holmes, Goldsmith, Fox, Yogananda, Cayce, *A Course in Miracles*, Quartus, or any other author or organization—and this search for understanding of another's Truth is vitally important in the awakening of your consciousness. But you can advance *vertically* only by embodying in consciousness that which is received from within you. It is only when you move into the realm of Self that you truly begin to climb that highest mountain.

Look at the symbol of the cross: †

The vertical line below the horizontal bar represents you as a seeker of Truth. The horizontal demarcation shows the process of study, research, contemplation of the teachings, meditation on the ideas presented, and the assimilation of the energy behind the words—all of which will open doors in consciousness and inspire you to take the inner journey toward the Secret Place. The vertical line above the bar represents this ascension into the Highest Aspect of your being where *your* guidance, *your* mission, and *your* Truth are revealed.

Translating all of this into principle, we would say that *Truth is dynamic, forever unfolding. To receive Truth, the mind must be unwrapped, challenged, and stretched. It then becomes receptive to the teachings of the Master within and serves as an open channel for the expression of the Divine Energies.*

Pointer No. 2: *There is only one of anything.*

In the Omnipresent Supreme Mind we call God, and which is individualized as our Divine Consciousness, are the archetypes of everything that exists in the phenomenal world. *Archetype* means "the original pattern from which all other things of the same kind are made." This gives us the starting point for changing energy into all manner of forms and experiences.

It is easy to say that we have everything and that we have it now, therefore we do not have any needs—and this is true on the inner plane, and would be in the outer if there were no blocks in consciousness. In the Absolute we understand that we are rich, whole, successful, and enjoying perfect relationships, but for ideal fulfillment in our incarnated physical plane lives we seek to release the Absolute into the relative. We want the invisible good that is ours by right of possession to become visible. We want tangible money in our hands, the radiant health in our bodies, the happy outcome of our ventures, and the loving bonds with people who are a part of our personal world. When our minds are clear for the expression of High Vision, the manifestation of the invisible into visibility is natural and automatic. And one way to open consciousness for the extension of energy into form is by understanding the Principle of Original Patterns and by putting that Principle into practice to fulfill our needs and desires.

What do you want to appear in your life at the present time? Think for a moment and make a mental note of all seemingly empty cups that you would like to see filled. In looking back over my life I have wished, hoped and prayed for a new career opportunity, a new home, new car, more money in the bank, a physical healing, the right book to write, the harmonizing of a relationship, the prospering of an organization, and so on. And gradually over the years I began to understand the Archetype Principle—that in my Divine Consciousness there is only one employer, one home, one car, one supply, one healing-healer-health, one book, one relationship, one organization, etc.

Let's phrase it this way: *The Original Patterns—the only one of anything—are in the form of pure Thought Energy impressed in the Mind of the God-Self within, and they work through your recognition and acknowledgement. As the Energy of a particular Pattern radiates through consciousness, consciousness will translate it into form and experience in direct accordance with what you can accept on the physical plane. The fewer inhibitions in consciousness, the greater and grander the manifestation.*

Is there a need for additional financial resources to meet your obligations? Then know that there is only one Supply, the Divine Thought-Pattern of Supply within you. Also bring to mind that the insufficiency is an ego belief in limitation to which you have given temporary power. But the ego is not Cause, Law, or Truth, so withdraw your judgement of appearances and focus on the presence within—on the One Supply that is the Truth of your being. Continue to meditate on this Truth until you feel the reality of your contemplation, and at that point you have made your connection with the Archetypal Energy of Abundance. Based on the statement of principle above, as the energy radiates through you, your consciousness will interpret and direct the energy to meet the needs of your particular situation at the highest level of your acceptance. How much can you accept? How vivid is your imagination? Just remember that the Energy of Self works in mysterious ways and knows all of the favorable circumstances in your world for the sudden appearance of money. You don't have to know the how and the way. Trust the Divine Ingenuity, and if there is anything for you to do to cooperate in the process you'll have a flash of intuitive guidance to do it. In the meantime, stretch your consciousness to accept only the highest, greatest, and grandest in life—and let the Master within do the rest.

Has a physical ailment flagged your attention? In the Mind of Self there are no imperfections, and a belief in sickness is nothing more than that—a belief. So you begin by changing your mind and believing the Truth that Healthfulness is the only Reality. You meditate on the Truth that God is the only Health there is, and you link up with the Original Pattern of Perfection—and you stay there until the Fire of Truth burns in your heart and the energy is released into the physical system.

If there is a "thing" that you need to enable you to function more effectively in the physical world, you become aware of its archetypal presence within and your consciousness will cast the energy into the proper form and act as a magnet to attract it into your life. I did not say that it would plop into your lap. You may have to leave the house or office to go buy it, but the decision as to where, when, what, and how much to pay will have been made for you, and you will instinctively know exactly what to do.

Whatever we desire, we already have, or we could not have desired it. Now we must realize that there is only one of anything, and work with that principle until it becomes our Truth and frees us from lack, limitation, disability, and discord.

Pointer No. 3: *Do not open yourself to Spiritual Truth unless you are willing to properly channel it.*

When Jan and I stepped on the spiritual path it was done with much secrecy. We did not talk to others about metaphysical principles and esoteric laws because we did not know if they would work, even though everything we read seemed to ring true in consciousness. As we began to apply the principles with a rush of enthusiasm, we found that our mental activity was greatly energized—as if our minds were saying "more, more, more!" We took the library and bookstores by storm, checking out and buying stacks of books at a time and reading at every available moment.

Soon our feeling natures began to be sensitized, adding steam to the boiler (power to consciousness), and within forty days after this introduction to Truth I had a very profound experience. It was February 1967, and I was driving from my office in Chicago to our home in the suburb of Wilmette. (We had left our home state of Texas ten years before to capture the pot of gold in the advertising business.)

The only way that I can describe the experience that night is to say that in a split second every fiber of my being took on the vibration of intense joy. It was as if every problem in my life suddenly vanished, all needs had been met, and Playtime-on-the-Planet had been declared for all the Divine Children by Father-Mother God. I had such an attack of happiness that I could hardly breathe, and if I had been stopped by a policeman he would have sworn I was on something. Fortunately I made it home in that totally zapped condition.

This had been a glorious infilling of the sacred energies, but I did not know at the time that everything received from within must be given for the benefit of others. As a Law of the Masters states it: "You have no right to receive that which you do not share."

For the next several years, which included a move back

to Houston, we went through a period of intense material accumulation, chronic spiritual pride, and a vibration in consciousness that could best be described as pompous selfishness. We did attend a New Thought church in Houston once in a while, but we quickly skipped out the nearest exit as soon as the services were over—no mingling, fellowship, loving, or sharing.

Now let me pause for a moment and go back to the spiritual principle. The crux of it is this: Once the door to consciousness is opened to receive the spiritual energies, the flow of that power must be for the good-of-all. The energies, of course, will make all things new for the individual who is experiencing the flow, but if the personality continues to focus only on its own personal desires and not on service to others, the flow will soon be blocked and the individual will be vulnerable to mental, emotional, and physical impairment. Nothing dreadful about this law. It is simply the way it works when the higher energies are bottled up and anchored in the personality. It's like spiritual constipation, and the effect in a person's life can be intense anger, greater self-centeredness, futility, guilt, a fear of relationships, a feeling of rejection and criticism from others, physical problems, financial insufficiency, and heightened disorder in the workplace.

While we may not have experienced all of the above we certainly had our share, and for a time I blamed it all on "chemicalization"—the idea of absorbing the new energies in an old state of consciousness and the resulting "shake-up" in an individual's world. That can be a problem, but in our case I realized that the cause of the turmoil was my attempt to hold and control the divine energy. The thoughts that were coming through emphasized my need to share, give, express! So I started with what I had "in the house"—the unfolding of my understanding of Truth. I began writing my "Thoughts on Truth" in a letter format, rented a mailing list of metaphysical enthusiasts and invited the people to subscribe to the monthly Letter. Out of a list of 5000, thirty-five people signed up, which showed me that humility can be a wonderful thing. Anyway, we later began our initial research for the book *The Superbeings*[1] and life moved into a more harmonious vibration.

Let's rephrase this particular principle in another way: *You cannot hoard spiritual energy for the exclusive use of the personality. It must be shared, given out, expressed, otherwise you will be transformed into bloated nothingness.* The Wisdom Teachings do not say it in exactly that way, but you get the idea. We could have speeded up our breakthrough even more if we had combined our research and the impersonal Truth sharing (the letters) with active involvement in a spiritual group—particularly one that was helping to heal the wounds of the planet and its people.

What do you have in the house? What do you have to share and express? Spiritual groups in your community would certainly welcome a new member, and your local New Thought church would greet a joyful uplifter of consciousness with open arms. The Quartus Society[2] would also love to have you play a part in its exciting adventure in the Light, and your involvement in the Planetary Commission's World Healing Day[3] each December 31st would be another way for you to give the world some of that high-vibration spiritual energy that you have been receiving from within. I know that from the moment that Jan and I announced this simultaneous global mind-link for the last day of each year, our lives have changed dramatically—and with your leadership participation, so will yours.

Think about what you have to give—whether it is your love, your joy, your understanding, your time, your dedication and support, your money—and find a place to give it. And while you should not cast your pearls of wisdom at everyone's feet, you might be more alert to the spiritual needs of others, counseling when appropriate or just listening to a friend in need. We should keep in mind that we did not come into this world as tourists. We came in to awaken to our True Identity, and as part of the memory-jogging exercise we accepted an assignment to help heal and harmonize Planet Earth. It is like a victim of amnesia returning to the town where he once lived, and to accelerate the remembering process he volunteers to help make the community a better place to live.

That is why we are here, and the express-or-suffer principle is one way of keeping us all on track in fulfilling our assignments. It is a failsafe device that keeps us headed in the right direction.

Pointer No. 4: *The Individual who denies that money is a spiritual asset is still working out of the lower nature of materiality.*

Many people who seek the spiritual way of life are living in insufficiency because they view money as separated from God and as a symbol of the satisfaction of personal desires. We must all realize that nothing is separate and apart from God—that money is spiritual substance made manifest, the creative energy of the Spirit stepped down into visibility.

The principle is this: *While working out of the lower nature in a vibration of materiality, money must be considered in material terms, otherwise it cannot be attracted to you, for like attracts like. However, once you are functioning on the Soul level in the spiritual vibration, money must be thought of as a great and powerful spiritual asset, otherwise it will not be attracted to you, for like attracts like.*

You have obviously chosen the spiritual way of life, so you should change your attitude regarding money and see it as the Energy of Divinity and an Expression of Love. Then your concept of the medium of exchange will be in accord with your Consciousness of Self, which opens the channel for manifestation.

Continuing with Pointers capsuled:

No. 5: *Energy follows thought, therefore, energy is the servant of mind and can be constructive or destructive in its expression. Are you healing or harming with your thoughts?*

No. 6: *If a teaching takes you away from a feeling of the Presence within—away from a reliance on Self—it is not Truth.*

No. 7: *In walking the Path, your faults, weaknesses and problems will become more evident to you. These are your repressions being lifted into the Light of Truth to be transmuted so that you will be a clearer channel for the Self's Divine Expressions. Welcome the cleansing with great joy.*

No. 8: *What you are seeing in others you are seeing in yourself.*

Change the way you look at yourself and you will see others differently. There is only one I.

No. 9: *The first step in attaining mastery is to learn how to love unconditionally. The Master within will teach the course, showing you how to be an open channel for God's Love.*

No. 10: *The Light Bearers are able to live simultaneously an inner and outer life, bringing their spirituality from within and extending it into the world of form and experience. This is the life of Heaven on Earth, which will be yours when you realize your True Identity.*

No. 11: *For the Kingdom to be manifest on Earth as it is in Heaven, it must come through your consciousness—and it will, just as soon as your personality is under the control of Self rather than ego.*

No. 12: *There is no such thing as failure. What we consider as failure is but a loss of time, yet in spiritual consciousness not even time can be lost.*

No. 13: *All disease and physical illness can be traced to inhibiting the Life Force radiating from the Master Self within. Shine as the Holy Sun and enjoy your radiant wholeness.*

No. 14: *You are not a physical body. You are the sum-total of all energies in expression as Pure Consciousness. You live above the physical vehicle, with the brain functioning as an apparatus to receive and transmit information received from your mind.*

No. 15: *The key to successful living may be summed up in one word: Harmlessness.*

No. 16: *You do not remove a partition and find another Self standing in the shadows. You simply awaken and find that you were It all the time.*

No. 17: *As a human being you script the play to create the experience to reveal the lessons. As a spiritual being the Master within lives through you, as you, and "experience" is no longer the teacher.*

No. 18: *When used with will and a controlled mind, the Spoken Word of Constructive Power can clear the consciousness channel of ego debris and accelerate the energy flow. Critical and destructive words create further obstructions to dam the flow.*

No. 19: *The first step in achieving freedom is to not take yourself so seriously.*

No. 20: *The second step is to cultivate a sense of humor.*

CHAPTER FIVE

The Energies of Will, Love, and Creative Intelligence

Thoughts and feelings establish vibrations in consciousness, and every thought—particularly ones with an emotional charge—gathers energy, for energy forever follows thought and adapts itself to the nature of the thought.

If you see your body, for example, as whole and perfect in your imagination, and *feel* that wholeness, you are creating a thought-form that will continually be fed with energy. Energy is life, power, and intelligence. Therefore, the thought-form comes alive as a powerful and perceptive entity conscious of itself (in this case) as a whole and perfect body. It was given birth in your consciousness, and there it will remain—growing, maturing, pulsating, serving you—unless later destroyed by you.

Because it is the nature of every living thing to seek out a vibration similar to its own, the thought-form begins to gravitate toward the Source of Life, the Central Sun of your Force Field, the Master Self within. In time it finds the Divine Counterpart, the perfect body Archetype established in God Mind. As the ideal meets the Real, a bridge is established enabling the currents of wholeness to flow through the centers to affect purification of the glands. If the imaged thought-form is not separated from the Divine Pattern of Perfection through a denial of wholeness, the circulation will continue and the healthfulness maintained.

You may, however, sometimes find it difficult to create a positive thought-form (whether of health, abundance, or relationships) and sustain it over a period of time, due primarily to the lack of mental-emotional discipline. In short, if you are not in control of your thoughts, emotions, and actions, then the images of wholeness, abundance, and harmony are likely to be shattered and the thought-form birthing process must begin anew. But the solution always precedes the problem, and the answer can be found in the Omnipotent Energy of God operating on three distinct vibrations in your Force Field.

These Energy Vibrations are Will and Purpose, Unconditional Love, and Creative Intelligence. In esoteric Wisdom, the one Energy in three movements of expression is often referred to as the Father, the Son, and the Holy Spirit.

While all outpourings of energy are keyed to the Seven Rays and Chakras, we should not be concerned with those aspects now. Rather, let's concentrate on the utilization of these three potent Forces as a means of controlling and focusing consciousness—because if we are not in control of our lives, our lives are out of control. Even the act of surrendering to Spirit is a conscious, decision-making step.

Employing the Energy of Will and Purpose

If you ever wake up in the morning feeling listless and uninspired, or if life seems to have no meaning for you and there is little motivation to move toward a goal, or if you find yourself floundering around with little self-discipline, then you need a good shot of the Power Energy of Will and Purpose. Here is a process that I have used to tap into it. In your imagination see a switch-plate marked **Energy of Will and Purpose**. Notice that the switch is in the OFF position. See yourself flipping the switch to ON and "hear" the sound deep within you—a hum similar to a generator starting up. Mentally connect with the radiating energy and feel the vibration. While you are using your imagination to activate the energy flow, this is not an imaginary exercise. The imaging-feeling action is literally directing the flow of energy through your system. Once you feel the radiation, speak these words with great enthusiasm:

The Power of God is working mightily in me now. I am hooked up to the Dynamo within and I am electrified with the Divine Energy of Will and Purpose.

I am quickened from head to toe, galvanized into action by the invincible currents flowing in and through me.

I am stirred, excited and thrilled over the opportunity this day to be and do and have according to the unlimited Vision of the Master Self I AM.

I no longer stand in my way, for I am God in expression, and God does not have obstacles or obstructions. My consciousness is on fire with will and purpose, and I am fired up!

I now go forth to joyfully accomplish my mission.

Work with this treatment until it takes, then go about your day with super inspiration. If you feel a drop, use this affirmation for a quick recharge:

I work powerfully and purposely for God, and my life is filled with wholeness, harmony, and abundance.

Also, be consciously aware that you are working with this awesome Energy. See the switch in the ON position throughout the day. Feel the power radiating through you and know that this Energy will support you and maintain your highest good while you are in tune with its vibration.

Employing the Energy of Unconditional Love

You *try* to be loving but you just do not feel like it. Sometimes it feels good to be angry, even though you know that you are probably going to have to suffer the consequences. Loving with no strings attached is fine for a Master, and you will do it when you have evolved to a higher state of consciousness, but there is no way that you are going to love Mr. Bigot or Miss Spiteful.

With this kind of attitude, protecting a positive

thought-form for health, wealth, and happiness is going to be just next to impossible. Since you cannot do it alone, why not call on the incredible Energy of Unconditional Love? The switch-plate is right there next to the other one. It is marked **Energy of Unconditional Love**—and the switch is in the OFF position. Reach into consciousness and flip it to ON. This time that sound you hear with your inner ear is like a musical tone, and that is *your* note that it is playing. Listen. . .and move deeply into consciousness to become one with the tone. Hear it spreading through your energy field. Now speak these words with passion:

God loves me. God loves me! Regardless of any mistake I have ever made, the Creator of Life loves me with all of Its Being. And since God loves me, how could I possibly not love myself?

Oh (state your name), I love you so! I love this me that is, the I that I AM, this self, this person, this mind, this spirit. My God! I am talking about You! When I love myself I am loving You! And when I love You I am loving myself, for we are eternally One. What a glorious Truth!

Now that I am aware again that Love is the Reality behind all form, I cannot love anything without loving everything. . .and so I do. I love everyone and everything everywhere. There are no conditions to this love, no qualifications. I am in love and love is in me and I let the glorious Love Energy pour through me now to heal every relationship and harmonize every situation in my life.

I am a radiating center of Divine Love. I feel it. I know it. I AM it! I now go forth into the world as the incredible Energy of Love!

To keep you on course during the day, use this short affirmation:

I work lovingly and easily for God, and my life is filled with wholeness, harmony, and abundance.

Again, keep the Love switch in the ON position, feeling the Love Vibration and hearing the Tone of Love playing in the depths of your consciousness.

Employing The Energy of Creative Intelligence

Your mind may seem so scattered that creative concentration is out of the question, and your vision of your role in the scheme of things so cloudy that you feel lucky to just see what is immediately in front of you to do. Creative visualization? Thoughtful contemplation? Forget it.

Obviously there is a deficiency of a particular energy vibration here, one called Creative Intelligence, which happens to be the power that sharpens the mental faculties.

There is a third switch-plate in consciousness, the one marked **Energy of Creative Intelligence**. It is OFF now; reach in and turn it ON. It sounds like the wind blowing through you, as if exhaling a deep breath, only continuous. Feel this gentle, whispering breath circulate through your mind. See it as a soft light expanding in your head, then moving down to your heart, on down to your solar plexus, radiating down your body and out all around you. Once you are centered in the light, speak these words with great feeling:

I see. I understand. I know. I AM. I mentally see the Truth within every so-called problem. I intuitively see the Reality behind every illusion. I thoughtfully see through every obstacle. I understand the Principle of Being. I know the absoluteness of the Law. I AM a spiritual being and I am free to BE according to my highest vision.

There is great clarity in my consciousness now as I view that which is before me to do. As a creator with God, I conceive and extend only the true thought-forms of wholeness, harmony, and abundance. I see myself living in a world of perfect peace, in a world filled with love and joy where the sense of separation from the Source is completely healed.

In my creative imagination I see myself as whole and healed, with an all-sufficiency of all things at all times. I see myself as loved and loving, unconditionally. I see myself as joyous, happy, and delighted to be me. I am on course now, poised, secure, and confident in the Light of Creative Intelligence.

And the affirmation to be used as a reminder during the day:

I work creatively and thoughtfully for God, and my life is filled with wholeness, harmony, and abundance.

Understand that the use of the Energies does not replace your meditations to deepen your spiritual consciousness. Being in tune with these vibrations should be thought of as a supplementary exercise to train consciousness to be deliberate, loving, and thoughtfully creative.

Once these characteristics are a part of your mental-emotional nature, you will find your spiritual work to be so much more effective. Reason: thought-forms based on spiritual Truth will be protected, and the manifestation channel will be kept clear of any obstructions that you might inadvertently place there. You apply the energies primarily to make your consciousness a fit place for God to work.

CHAPTER SIX

The Pure Light
of Intuition

During a period of quietness following meditation, I received a message from within that spoke of the difference between emotional feeling and intuitive knowing. I assumed that this information came through because I had been contemplating "right decision-right action" regarding a long range vision that I had seen. And while the scenario dealt with the future, I had felt that plans should be formulated and I was preparing myself for instinctive action from the highest aspect of consciousness. What came to me was something like this:

"The Way is not shown through emotions but through the higher Mind, through the faculty of intuition. Feelings can be misleading for they are often reactions from the lower self. Even a sentimental emotion disguised as love can be an improper stimulus for action.

"A strong personal desire can also evoke an emotional response, which would be interpreted as a divine signal to move toward the goal, even while the higher Mind is suggesting a different plan of fulfillment. From this, one may perceive that mind rather than emotions represents the path of guidance. Yes, but the mind, too, may represent a pitfall, for mental reasoning and analytical thinking have only an affinity for past mental impressions, or the creation of new thought-forms cast out of recycled astral energy, in other words, the building of illusion out of illusion.

"To be instinctively guided along life's path, an individual must move above the emotions, above the rational mind, up to the knowing faculty—a point of Light emanating from the Higher Self. This Light is intuitional understanding. It is illumination. It is ever-present radiating energy which leads to omniscience in the latter days of the spiritual journey."

After pondering these ideas for a time, it seemed to me that the consciousness that is receptive to the clear light of intuition may be described as centered, detached, impersonal, quiet but alert, open to revelation, and focused in the now.

To experience your knowing faculty, come into balance and ask yourself, "What do I intuitively believe?"—about some point of interest in the phenomenal world. Then see the reality that is presented to your mind's eye, the clear vision that is expressed as an inner knowing. You may also wish to distinguish between lower pressing and higher piloting through another exercise. Bring into mind a particular situation or circumstance in which you find yourself, then ask the following questions and write the response:

1. What do I emotionally feel is the way to reconcile this matter?

2. What does my logical, reasoning mind tell me to do about this matter?

3. What do I intuitively know about my role in the outcome of this matter?

The objective of these questions is to solicit a response from your emotions, your thinking apparatus, and your intuitive nature. The key is to monitor your feelings and measure your thoughts through the pure energy of intuition to achieve the highest level of guidance. As an example, back in the early 1970s I was about to merge my company with another organization—which logic told me was the most reasonable thing to do—yet I intuitively knew that it was not the best course of action over the long haul. I let reason sway me and went ahead with the plan, much to my later regret. The chemistry of the two companies was not the right mix and "explosions" soon became the order of the day.

I am now finding that the more detached and impersonal I am in making choices, the greater the knowingness of "right decision-right action." Sometimes we just have to get ourselves out of the way so that the Light of Self can show us the way. And then, in a very mystical sense, we literally become the way.

Here is a meditation that will be helpful in opening your faculty of intuition.

I am poised and powerful in the Presence of God.

My emotional nature is quiet, my mind is still, and I am one with my All-Knowing Self.

Detached from this world, impersonal to illusion, I am totally open to the Divine Revelations from above.

From the radiance illuminating my mind I see only Reality.

From the celestial note issuing forth from the Highest Realm of my Being, I hear only Harmony.

From the stream of crystal clear essence pouring into my consciousness from on High, I know only the Truth.

From the pure Light of Intuition I know the Way.

I am now able to take direct and correct action.

I know what to do, how to do it, and when.

I am a Divine Knower.

My Knowingness now reveals the Plan and my part in it.

I watch. I listen. I wait.

I see. I hear. I know.

I now move forward to accomplish that which is mine to do.

CHAPTER SEVEN

The Den of Lions

Since this is really Daniel's story, I will let him tell it in his own words, as I might hear it in my imagination.

Daniel: In these latter days of the twentieth century, my experience in the lion's den is being replayed time and time again in people's lives all over the world. I was victorious because I had placed God first in my life and let everything else be of secondary importance. I refused to compromise my spiritual integrity and held firm to the courage of my convictions. But people today believe that they are being eaten alive by the stock market, economic manipulations, the seeming impersonal force of nature, disease, and by the fear of what is around the next corner. And all the time they could have shut the lion's mouths if they had not broken their devotion to God, the Holy Self within.

To help you understand how you can be protected from anything and everything in the phenomenal world I will give you the details of my experience, which you can superimpose over your particular situation.

First, you must realize that nothing ever happens by chance. Every activity in the physical world can be traced to an activity in consciousness, individual or collective. At the beginning of the Persian rule over Babylon I was one of the three presidents reporting directly to Darius the king. The atmosphere or general feeling of the time was very emotional, with constant fears about one thing or another, and what you call "channeling" was widespread throughout the land. Because of the intense influence from the astral plane essentially everyone was in the predicting business, and no aspect of life or society was immune. Messengers from the seers were constantly forecasting severe economic problems, war, plagues, and natural catastrophes—much as the media is doing today. The result was confusion among the general populace, chaotic conditions, and total attention directed to the outer material world. With this kind of collective consciousness, you can readily see that the people were setting themselves up for self-fulfilling prophecies.

One day I encountered a merchant, and with great animation he talked of a foretold collapse of the empire. And I said, "What is it to you? Your support is not in the marketplace; it is from God within, your true Self, and unless you realize this you will lose all that you possess." And he walked away, shaking his head in mockery at my admonition.

Later, while with a group of artisans, a spokesman queried me about the prophecies of flood, fire and quakes in the land, and I said, "Are you not already drowning in intolerance, filled with the fires of hatred, and quaking with fear of the future? These things shall surely come to pass to prove that your tomorrow is but an extension of what you accept as true today. Go within and seek the Holy Presence. Ponder your Truth and you will find that in the Presence of God there is an eternal defense against nature's cleansing force." They did not listen.

As one in authority at that time I was able to speak freely, and while I did not force my views on others I did attempt to guide minds and hearts into a higher way of thinking and feeling. I wanted to teach them the secret of the *I*—that Point of Omnipresence within each soul that knows Itself to be God as Individual being. I tried to tell them that if they would but open the door of consciousness to receive the Presence, and if they would embody the Spirit of God, the activity of Spirit would appear as every needed thing in their lives. God is individual Selfhood, I told them, and all that they could ever seek or desire in an eternal lifetime is contained with the I. But, I said, they must live in the I *as* the I—and then by adding only one word is the Identity grounded in Earth to subdue it and transform it into Heaven. That word is **AM**, and because **I AM** encompasses the infinite All and brings It into the Now, the individual who recognizes the **I AM** *has* All Now!

So many times I tried to make it clear that since the All-That-Is is within, it cannot be found in the without. Peace and protection cannot be found in the outer world. Wellness cannot be discovered on the third-dimensional plane. Even money obtained through material manipulation cannot be sustained. It is only when the man or woman seeks to demonstrate the Truth of God and not the distortion of materiality will the spell be broken—the spell of devastation, disease, and limitation.

It was said that I was distinguished above the other presidents because I had realized my divine nature, and the king planned to set me over the whole kingdom. Now, until such time as the Christos is liberated and the planetary consciousness is predominantly spiritual, the aggregate of humanity's lower nature—the mass ego—ever seeks a denial of the Divine Reality. Perhaps I could say that there is an initiation in the life of every committed seeker where he or she must demonstrate spiritual integrity. If the principle is compromised, the next expansion in consciousness is delayed. If one stands firm in Truth, however—regardless of the seeming consequences—a giant step is taken up the evolutionary ladder.

In my case, the other two presidents conceived a scheme to trick King Darius and have me cast into a den of lions. They knew that I prayed and meditated daily, and they took this devotion into consideration in establishing an ordinance that "whoever makes petition to any god or man for thirty days except to King Darius shall be cast into the den of lions."

When the king signed the document I immediately went home, got down on my knees, prayed and gave thanks before my God, as was my daily custom. My adversaries were waiting and watching, and they quickly reported to Darius that I had violated the ordinance and must be fed to the lions.

At this point let me explain that when you go through any initiation leading to expansions in consciousness, there are always advocates on both sides of the veil working on your behalf—assisting you in strengthening your will and purpose in moving through the initiation. I had made my decision to hold to Principle when I defied the order not to pray to God for thirty days. This action put out a silent call, so to speak, to all who would support my decision, and one of those responding was King Darius himself.

The king was much distressed when he heard that I was going to be fed to the lions, but my adversaries reminded him that any ordinance established by the king could not be changed. The king could do nothing to free me, yet at the den he spoke Words of Power on my behalf. He said, "May your God, whom you serve continually, deliver you!" Then the king went to his palace and fasted through the night—another act of loving support.

The night spent with the Lions was really most pleasant. I made contact with the feeling nature of those magnificent animals almost instantly and connected us all in a vibration of love. I was able to do this because I had daily lived my Truth. The realization of the Spiritual I of my being was more important than anything else in my life, so I was prepared in consciousness for the experience. I knew there was no power in effects, that my protection was the power of God appearing as my shield, and that my radiation of love was God in expression as the harmonizing influence. Without this attunement with my Self, I surely would have been devoured by the hungry lions.

Now, what about you? In this present and quickly changing world, will you come out of the darkness of the cave in one piece? Have you dedicated your life to the realization of your Divine Identity, or are you satisfied living in a sea of uncertainty? Are you looking at trends and prophecies with fear and trepidation, or do you see only opportunities for transmutation? Are you relying only on Spirit to appear as every needed thing, or are you still trying to manipulate material conditions? Are you ready to prove your spiritual integrity against all odds—even to the mouths of lions—or will you take the easy way out and deny your Truth? Do you understand that you have a loving support group that will assist you along every mile on the journey Home, or are you resigned to being lost and alone on the Path?

The lions are waiting for your answer.

CHAPTER EIGHT

Being Born Anew

When the Truth of Who and What we really are begins to dawn in us, those first faint rays of recognition are felt in the heart, and the birthing process commences, leading ultimately to the fusion of the Self and the personality.

What is meant by the *heart*? The Bible has 169 references to "heart"—and in the Ancient Wisdom literature the heart is considered to be of extraordinary importance. Are the mystics and masters referring to a physical organ? No, for the body is not the cause of anything. Are they pointing to our emotional system? No, the etheric center (chakra) corresponding to the solar plexus is the instrument through which the emotional energy flows. Are they talking about our feeling nature? To some extent, yes, but the major emphasis is on an Energy Center that is the source of the most awesome power of the universe.

The heart center is the fourth or middle chakra in the chain of seven located within the lines of force that make up the etheric body. Where the lines of force cross each other, they form great "whirlpools" for the distribution of energy. And each of the seven major centers (chakras) receives a *specialized* energy from the Central Core of Being, the Master Self, for circulation through the individual's Force Field. The heart chakra is considered the "Agent" of

Self, and serves as the outlet for the extension of energy into the phenomenal world and the manifestation of form. Whatever we consider good, true, and beautiful in life must come through the heart center if it is to have any degree of permanency in our individual worlds. It is also the focal point where emotions are transmuted into the feelings of unconditional love, and is the place where the "Christ Idea" of our Divine Identity is born. This is the first initiation into higher consciousness, the acceptance of our Truth of Being.

What are we to do to avail ourselves of this passageway between Heaven and Earth? First, we should understand the dynamics of this Power Center. We are told in the Bible that "the Lord looks on the heart" (1 Sam. 17:7). This means that the focus of our Holy Self is on this "lotus" in a concentrated gaze of loving knowingness. "And I will give them one heart, and put a new spirit within them." (Ex. 11:19) "I will put my law within them, and I will write it upon their hearts." (Jer. 31:33) Here we see that right within the vortex where the powers of God unite and spirit and matter join is the *universal* production facility (the *one* heart) for everything that appears in our lives. And it is under the direction of the "new spirit"—"new" because it is the nature of our Self being reborn. This Spirit of Truth formed in us represents the law of the Lord-Self—"law" being the spiritual principles of life that are impressed (written) on the heart.

In *Esoteric Healing*[1] the Tibetan Master, D.K., says that "the heart centre corresponds to the 'heart of the Sun,' and therefore to the spiritual source of light and love. . .and (the heart's) transforming, magnetic and radiatory power is essential for the reconstruction of the world." Yes!—the reconstruction of our individual worlds as the illusions are dissolved and Reality revealed.

Manly Hall says that "the spiritual nature is most commonly symbolized by the heart. . .all the Mysteries recognized the heart as the center of spiritual consciousness." Hall also writes that in each one of us "the innermost and the outermost spheres are connected by a gate which leads from the not-self and its concerns to the Self and its realizations. . .this gate is the heart. . ."[2]

And let's remember that "as he thinketh in his heart, so is he." (Prov. 23:7) When we think with the heart, with thoughts clothed in love, we are in tune with the Higher Mind—"I commune with my heart in the night." (Ps. 77:6) How do we bring in that Higher Mind to dramatically transform our world? By meditating on the Great Self within, which connects us with the Gaze and fills our heart center with the Truth that sets us free.

In this regard think of the heart as a circle of light that expands with every degree of Self recognition, ever enlarging to accommodate more and more of the Divine Incarnation. If we just *talk* about our Inner Reality all the time, the problems and challenges will continue to be concretized. But as we become truly *conscious* of the Indwelling Presence, things begin to happen, and with every step we take in consciousness toward the Ultimate Merger, the faster and more complete is the transformation.

Let your Holy Self be formed in your heart. As you contemplate the Divine Presence, more of that Presence is formed in the substance of this Power Center. *This is the new Birth*; it is being born anew. This is the Kingdom that comes, the Daily Bread that satisfies every hunger. At first it is only a child in the manger, only a light of the Kingdom, a small slice of the Bread of Life. But in this child is all the power of God, in that light is the Sun of Miracles, and in that slice is eternal manna from Heaven.

Fill your heart with a conscious awareness of your Master Self as the answer to every problem, the fulfillment of every need—as the Source, Energy, and Activity of every form, condition, situation, and experience in your life. And as that recognition builds in the Love Center and radiates out to encompass your world, you will see it as it was in the beginning. . .a time of wholeness, abundance, joy, and peace.

Begin now. Look within and feel the radiant Splendor of your Lord Self reaching down and touching your Love Center, and bow your head to the point of that feeling and behold the Wonder Child. Cross your arms over your heart and pay homage to this Magnificent One Who heals all your infirmities, casts out the demons of ego, feeds the multitudes, stills the tempest, provides the money for the Tribute, and turns the waters of negation into the fruits of a life more abundant. Express your love for this Angel of the Presence, and make a commitment now to care for this Light of your world with devoted attention and overflowing love.

Can you now express "joy to the world"? The Lord *is* come!

CHAPTER NINE

All the Good in Life
is Natural

Before we move on to Part II and the manifestation process, I feel that it is vitally important for us to understand that we do not have to manifest or create anything. The Cosmos is forever in automatic expression, manifesting all that it is—and out of Super Abundance, Super Wholeness, and Super Life can only come that same Super Nature. Therefore, it is only *natural* to be rich, radiantly healthy, and enjoying life to the fullest. To be otherwise is *unnatural*. To be poor, sick, and depressed means that we have increased the amount of resistance in our electrical circuitry—and the higher the resistance, the less the flow of the Divine Currents.

The entire Universal Energy Field is electric and everything that is manifest is electrical. Science knows this, but what it doesn't tell us is that each individual energy field is composed of nothing but flowing electricity. And the electricity follows the Divine Circuits (Spiritual Patterns) to manifest forms and conditions matching the absolute quality of the Source. The electrical power flowing through us never thinks of anything but giving to the fullest measure of its capability, which is infinite, and all of its circuits have been designed to handle the full high voltage flow. It knows nothing about those things in consciousness that resemble switches, fuses, or rheostats. The power is only conscious of being all that it is.

If any one individual was sufficiently transparent in consciousness with no limitations imposed, and was completely clear of personal ego, he or she could pay off the national debt tomorrow with a surplus left over to bail out all of the other nations. The physical body would be so perfect that it would appear ethereal, and consciousness so ecstatic that life would be nothing less that a rapturous adventure in all that is good, true, and beautiful. But that writer in the Old Testament knew about the unnatural condition that we had imposed on human consciousness, and how dedicated we are in limiting the Great Unlimited.

In Malachi 3:10 we read: "prove me now herewith, saith the Lord of Hosts, if I will not open you the windows of heaven and pour you out a blessing, that *there shall not be room enough to receive it*. The italicized words tell us that we have closed ourselves down to such an extent that we cannot handle all that the Universe is trying to give us. The blessing is so immense that human consciousness cannot accept it; it is so vast and stupendous that it is immeasurable to the human-conditioned mind. Imagine, the Unlimited Expressions of Infinite Being saying to this Absolute-All-That-Is, "I'm sorry, but I just can't accept my inheritance, my estate, my birthright. I'm simply not worthy of such an endowment, and therefore I must close the door on you and accept my limitations." No wonder we live in an asylum.

The Divine Currents flowing from on High enter our auric field to produce Light, Heat, and Power. *Light is Illumination*, the Central Spiritual Sun focused as the brilliance of knowledge, wisdom, and understanding. *Heat is Love*, the Cause behind all manifestation, the Cosmic Fire that creates new form and vivifies all things. *Power is Will and Purpose*, the authority to work in and with all energies to keep the circuits open and the magnetic force intact. With Illumination, Love, and Will there is nothing we cannot do, be, or have—yet we continually live with gaps in the circuit, which stop the flow of the creative currents.

Looking at electricity in the mundane sense, the flow of

electric current depends on its pressure, rate, and the resistance of the conductor to the flow. In the spiritual dimension, the Divine Electrical Thrust (pressure) is absolute, unconditional, and unlimited. Its velocity (rate) is total and maximum—so infinitely faster than the scientific calculation of the "speed of light" that its Creative Energy is perpetually working in the *now*. Therefore, the pressure and rate are forever in a state of perfect, permanent, and unfailing *givingness*. That leaves only one factor as the culprit—the resistance of the conductor, i.e. the resistance in consciousness.

Tracking down the opposition

There are many reasons why we have switched off the current, caused breaks in the circuit with fuses, and dimmed the light with our self-created rheostats. One is through ignorance of our Truth of Being. We assumed that we were less than Divine—that we were condemned, victimized humans—and we consented to play that role on the stage of life. But thousands of years ago this lie was exposed, and on some level of consciousness within each individual the Truth is known. Of course, it may be so deeply buried that only the animal nature is expressed, but even in this tomb of darkness the spark of salvation is working, and someday those sealed vaults will open and awakened ones will emerge. There are also millions of people on the planet now who have at least an intellectual understanding of Spiritual Reality, and while they may continue to function as people with amnesia, they believe that the Truth is true and are working daily to awaken to their former state of Consciousness. And there are still others who have moved up the evolutionary ladder to the point of *realization*, where the Truth is known, and they are living as full cooperators with the Universal Will-To-Good. So we cannot continue to point the finger at the mental darkness of the human race as our excuse for not living in Reality.

The crux of the problem, in my opinion, is in our sense of priorities. It comes down to what is truly important to us, and for some, living in the dark night of the soul is the perfect place to be. In such self-created experiences we do not have to take responsibility for our scarcities, unemployment, sickness, or strained relationships. We can say, "Well, you know, I'm going through another one of those dark nights of the soul, and I'll just keep on keeping on until this passes and I see the light again." And we speak such words with our hand on the light switch.

Knowing that any kind of darkness in life has been caused by our own resistance in the circuits, it seems to me that we have the responsibility to make the necessary adjustments in consciousness, using whatever tool is available. If it has to do with a blown fuse in another life, then let's go back to that incarnation and make the correction through understanding. I have seen the reason for, and the opportunity to heal, old wounds from long ago, thus giving me a boost on the spiral toward ultimate freedom. If it takes a greater comprehension of the energies and forces impacting us, then we have the obligation to learn about the causal powers and how they work in consciousness to bind or free us. Jan and I have had major breakthroughs by identifying the living energies within and working to withdraw ego projections from these twenty-two archetypes that we call "Angels."[1] We have also devoted countless hours to meditating on the Holy Master Self to draw more of the Spiritual Consciousness into personality, and have used a broad variety of other techniques and formulas to open the flow. And in every situation we discovered new and powerful expressions of Light, Heat, and Power. I am not trying to set us up as role models; I am simply pointing out that each one of us has some personal work to do in clearing consciousness, and we must not neglect that responsibility.

To say, "The dynamic flow of wisdom, love, and will through me is my all-sufficiency" is true, but such statements may have little effect on the jammed circuits. And surrendering everything to the corrective action of Spirit requires a willingness that may not suddenly spring forth from the subconscious level. Even bringing in the purifying Fire of Spirit to burn away false beliefs and error patterns calls for a degree of faith and acceptance that may be beyond our state of consciousness at the time. Let's remember the axiom that "God helps those who help themselves." To seek the kingdom first where all things will be added means to enter into a dedicated activity of seeking, searching, knocking, and exploring to find the crossed wires and repair the circuits—and we do this with an open mind. If a particular process does not fit our present belief system, it may be just the one to knock out the resistance factor, once we get rid of our prejudices.

You may have noticed that our spiritual research to "get the bloated nothingness out of the way of the divine circuits" is not limited to only the traditional processes. If it takes an unconventional approach, that could make it even more exciting. In fact, it was in our study of the interplay of energies and forces—archetypal and planetary—that we discovered what we now consider the basic flaw in essentially all human electrical systems, which when corrected, would no longer impede the Divine Currents.

The Primary Obstruction

Our discovery of the major resistance was found in *relationships*. Wherever there is any form of relationship, regardless of how casual or intense—whether with family, friends, associates in the workplace, even strangers—the law of cause and effect is in its most accelerated mode of action and reaction, casting a glaring light on the entire sowing and reaping process. With every action in thought, word, and deed there is a compensating action, which becomes a cause for further action, which leads to additional reaction, and on and on throughout the universe.

This is the principle of "karma." Karmic causes did not come into play until the universe was thrown out of balance with the sense of separation—the dream of being separated from God and the formation of physical bodies. When the consciousness of unity and oneness of all life faded, the phenomenon of "relationships" came into being. The law of cause and effect became a part of the natural process at that time in order to restore universal equilibrium. It does this by bringing into balance through compensating factors every action for which we are responsible. On the outer scene we learn wisdom through experience; on the inner plane perfection continues because the law has "thrown off" the discord to be harmonized in the universal karmic process.

In tracking these karmic effects through case histories of various individual situations, we see that in essentially every case of scarcity, sickness, accident, disappointment, failure, and unemployment, the faulty switch in the circuitry reflects a problem in one or more relationships—real or imagined. In each situation, physical, emotional and mental energy was used to generate causes which threw things out of balance, resulting in a compensating force being returned to the sender.

Look at where you are in life at this moment. You know that all the good in life is natural and automatic—that you have been given all that you could possibly desire for the most magnificent life imagined—yet you may be continuing to experience a shortage of supply, sickness in the body, unfulfillment in life, and other conditions that are contrary to the Divine Purpose and Standard. If you are, scan your consciousness to see and feel any relationship blips—husband, wife, son, daughter, father, mother, friends, acquaintances, associates (present and former), anyone and everyone on this side of the veil and beyond. A strong, hot, emotionally reactive blip tells you that you are generating a force that will ultimately return to you as some kind of an imbalance in your life. Even a faint, barely discernable echo may be the tip of the iceberg, with the great mass of judgement, condemnation, and resentment well below the surface. Yet it is still setting in motion a decree that you will eventually have to deal with.

With this understanding, Jan and I have begun to look at situations from a triangular approach. The top point of the triangle is the perceived problem. The left bottom point is the energy involved, and the right point is the relationship block. Here are a few composite examples, summarized and simplified.

For years Frank experienced financial difficulties. Even with good money management he never had enough at any one time to meet his financial obligations. The energy involved here is the energy of supply, or abundance, and it was being screened out through discord in the family. Based on childhood memories of not being able to fully meet his mother's expectations, Frank grew up with a subconscious memory bank filled with feelings of being inept, incompetent, and ineffective. He projected these aspects of himself on to his wife and son and became severely critical of their "constant bungling"—resulting in a highly hostile home environment that produced even more guilt and anger. In time, Frank learned that the energy of abundance is the energy of love and goodwill, and he began to understand that every time he denied a full measure of those qualities to others, the rheostat would go into operation to increase the resistance in the circuit. He also recognized that what he had been judging in others was what he was condemning in himself. Through love and forgiveness of that part of himself, he was able to find peace within and restore harmony in the home. It was not long before his consciousness opened to allow the supply to flow in its own natural way.

Doris was one of those (to use her words) "terribly unfulfilled" people who walk through life with head held low, and her daily chatter was about moving to another town to find greater happiness in life. What she did not realize at the time was that (1) we take our consciousness with us wherever we go, and (2) she was misusing the energy of divine order. This is the energy that produces joy in life and works naturally and automatically to express peace, poise, and confidence. How was the energy being diffused? By her constant criticism, put-down, and rejection of her husband, Tom. It was not until she learned that all husbands and wives are each other's "Shadow" did the healing process begin. The Shadow is our alter-ego representing everything about ourselves that we ever repressed, and our partner in life represents the Shadow's projection. What Doris was actually seeing in Tom was her masculine self as a complete bore—less spiritual than the feminine, unenlightened, naive, and an unworthy companion in life. One she understood that side of herself, made peace with it and withdrew the projections from Tom, she found a new sense of joy in life. The fulfillment that she was seeking came *naturally* through a new career opportunity, stimulating new friends, and a renewed love affair with Tom.

Wayne had spent most of his adult life either unemployed or underemployed, never seeming to get into the groove of "right livelihood." Obviously the energy of success was being shut down. In tracing this to a possible relationship problem, Wayne finally realized that he was very apathetic regarding intimate family relationships, and that he carried this attitude even further as far as friends were concerned. He admitted that his life was almost completely self-oriented, that he was satisfied without interaction with others, and was not inspired to develop close personal relationships—except with some people who lived at a distance. (No sudden invasion of privacy.) At the root of a lethargic, self-satisfied mind that opposes the cultivation of right relations is a fear of being dominated by others, which blocks energy that naturally expresses as achievement, advancement, good fortune and happy outcomes. Wayne has now begun to appreciate what true family bonding means, and he's also starting to reach out to others in his community—striving to develop and maintain real and lasting friendships. As the energy of success is released, whole new fields of opportunity will open to him, including his True Place in life.

Physical dis-ease can also be traced to attitudes and actions in relationships. Generally speaking, allergies relate to a misuse of the energy of loving relations—being touchy and oversensitive because of feelings of low self-esteem. Cancer deals with a block in the energy of unconditional love, caused by self-pity, grief, and resentment in personal relations. Diabetes may result from a misuse of the energy of discernment through impulsive behavior and the desire to control relationships. Heart problems may occur because of a block in the energy of strength, thus producing a "struggle-through-life" state of mind that repels productive and rewarding relationships, leading to further futility. Lung problems relate to the energy of loving relations and the grief experienced through the improper choice of a love partner, and the subsequent ending of the relationship. Stomach and intestinal problems can often be traced to a block in the energy of wisdom, frequently caused by irrational acts in relationships and emotional instability; also by an indifference to the emotional needs of others.

The Power Plant Within

From the Blazing Sun of Love within, the all-inclusive Rays shine forth to express the Unlimited All-Good. It is our Self fulfilling Itself through us, and our consciousness is the acceptor, the transformer, and yes, the limiter. Our Loving Holiness says, "All that I have is yours, and I am eternally giving all that I am to you." How much can we accept? By our own decisions, how much of the finished kingdom will be transformed into incompleteness? How many limitations must we place on the infinite givingness?

It is absolutely true that the Spirit of the Essential Self will help to clear Its channel of expression through the energy of forgiveness and love, and without a doubt all karmic debts can be dissolved by a sufficient rise in consciousness. But we will not be open to that love and cannot reverse the laws of mental and emotional gravity until we take the necessary steps in this world to clean up our mess. This was spelled out very clearly in John 5:17—"My Father is working still, and I am working." It must be a cooperative effort of conscious mind and Master Self working together. Through our attunement with Self we can be guided every step of the way. We can be shown the hot spots in every relationship and how we "relate" to (meaning interaction with) God, Self, our own personality, people in general, and every kind of person who comes into the range of our consciousness. We can be taken into the past to see where we initiated karmic causes, and on the screen of our mind we can view every situation where we cast true or false bread upon the waters of life. But the decision to become totally involved in this healing process is ours, and we must take the initiative to follow through with action.

Since the energy involved in relationships is the stuff that resistance is made of, it seems to me that a top priority would be to get ourselves clear and clean. Personally, I want to take advantage of the Infinite Good in life that is natural and automatic, and I would like to get to the point where there would be enough room in my consciousness to receive all of the blessings poured from the windows of heaven. If you are on the same wavelength, please join me in a new commitment to heal every relationship that is a part of our consciousness.

Make a list of everyone who could possibly trigger even a trace of irritation. Look at the anger, the hurt, the disappointment, the resentment, the judgement—and understand that you are condemning yourself. Then isolate that disliked part of yourself that you have projected on others and take it into the Light of Spirit to be loved, forgiven, and healed. This enables you to give up resentment toward everyone (the meaning of forgiveness) and restore harmony in your world. And if you are led to take a specific action on the physical plane in a one-on-one encounter to further harmonize the situation, do it.

Remember that you are not trying to create, change, or improve anything in the physical world; you are not trying to get something that is not already there. All that you are attempting to do is get into the flow of the natural process— and do what comes *naturally*. If you do not want more money in your life, that is your decision, but do not forget that over one billion people live in absolute poverty, and the Universe is seeking suitable channels to relieve this inequality. As stated in the *World Goodwill Newsletter*[2], "Money is to the life of the planet what the circulatory system is to the life of the body. And just as there is dis-ease in the body when that circulation is congested or blocked, so there is dis-ease on the planet when money is hoarded and imprisoned by attitudes of fear, distrust, selfishness, greed and materialism. Increasingly money as enlightened energy will become the instrument of our goodwill, insuring more speedy progress towards the health and well-being of all."

If you have decided to live with your ailments in some sort of a masochistic comfort zone, that is your choice. But remember that the healing and wholeness of the physical body is important if we are to carry out our part of the Divine Plan. We need to be "in shape" to reveal the *natural* world of peace, love, forgiveness, and understanding. And we have the responsibility to live life to the fullest during this incarnation as an example and inspiration to others—so that they, too, may awaken to Heaven on Earth as a Natural Reality.

As that Higher Part of me has said so many times, "It's fun to be healthy, wealthy, and fully alive." That is true. After all, it's only natural.

PART II

The Manifestation Process

Introduction to
Part II

As you incorporate the ideas and concepts contained in
Part I of this book and deepen your knowledge of spiritual
principles, you are building a foundation in consciousness
for a new life of love, joy, peace, and fulfillment. Some
readers will find that only a slight adjustment in mind is
necessary to reveal the Reality of wholeness and
abundance that has been there all the time, simply
obscured by the fog of misunderstanding. For others, there
may be a completely new awareness of a greater and higher
I and a joyous excitement that there is nothing that you
cannot do, be, or have—yet the appearances in the outer
picture will seem fixed and not dramatically affected by
prayer, meditation, and self-healing action. And the
reason is that consciousness has not yet shifted into the
higher vibration.

To those who can identify with this condition, let me
assure you that there is a way to move beyond the lacks
and limitations of the third-dimensional plane while still
being influenced by the "human" energies of the lower
nature. What is required is an elevation of consciousness
to activate a precise sequence of mind actions, resulting in
a clear channel for the manifestation. Of course, the fullness of the demonstration and its degree of permanency

will depend on the *altitude* achieved in consciousness and the *attitude* maintained in mind. A fearful outlook can cancel out the manifestation; a positive one can hold it in place. But nothing ventured, nothing gained, so let's reach for the stars and keep reaching until the grip is strong and firm.

We are all evolving into that state of consciousness where miracles are routine and positive changes occur without "taking thought." This is our destiny, but we do not have to wait until we are fully awakened to enjoy the good things in life. Wherever we are on the path, we can prove the principles and the power now through conscious, intentional, and deliberate action. This is *voluntary cooperation*, as distinguished between a creative activity that is occurring from the Self-acting movement of the Higher Consciousness independent of personality. In one case the operation is "manual"—in the other it is "automatic"—and if we have to shift gears manually for a time until our consciousness expands to the spontaneous mode, let's be patient in our awakening and grateful that we have the authority now to fulfill our dreams of a life more abundant.

One method of voluntary cooperation is through the use of a ten-step program to duplicate the vibrations of spiritual consciousness. Our research has revealed that consciousness is in reality an individualized energy field—a force field of concentrated spiritual energy—and if we are not enjoying the abundant life in all aspects, it is because the vibrations within this energy field are out of tune. When these vibrations are raised to the proper tone and pitch, consciousness becomes harmonically balanced and wholeness and well-being are outpictured in a person's life and affairs.

By way of illustration, think of the frequencies within each energy field as similar to the strings on a harp, with each string corresponding to a particular law or principle in the creation of form in the physical world. When each string, so to speak, is vibrating at the correct or divine frequency, the consciousness is harmonious and clear, and visible forms and experiences are created out of invisible substance. We call this activity "the manifestation process."

Jan and I began developing a specific spiritual treatment based on this process after reviewing the consciousness characteristics of the various awakened ones we encountered. In looking for the common denominators, we found that they were all in tune with their divine center, or God Self, and in practicing the Presence of God they had drawn forth their Truth of Being into the heart center—into the fullness of their thinking and feeling natures. Under divine authority this spiritual consciousness began to exercise its will to choose that which would be expressed in the particular individual's life, and whatever was chosen or decreed by this Truth Consciousness was automatically accepted by the subjective mind and registered as a sense or feeling of *have*.

This is all a simultaneous action where consciousness anticipates every possible need in the physical world, chooses divine fulfillment, accepts it, and through acceptance expresses the conviction of having it. And it is through this knowledge of *have* that the awakened ones image fulfillment as a present reality—and they see with such intensity of imagination and love that the normal timeframe for visible manifestation is greated reduced. (Jesus could *instantly* bring form ideas into visibility.)

With the understanding that what can be seen in the mind's eye is a *now* experience, the activity of the law (spiritual mind action) is automatically called into play and the invisible substance begins to take shape as the particular form, situation or experience desired. What has happened during this imaging phase of the process is that the spiritual mind has said, in effect, "I see the fulfillment, therefore it is done." And this declaration of consciousness has signaled the action of God, the impersonal Power, to take over and complete the demonstration.

At this point consciousness moves into a surrender mode—a letting go—a total releasing of the will to the Higher Power to do its perfect work. And since spiritual consciousness knows that only the highest and greatest good is now coming into visibility, there is a joyous feeling of gratitude and thanksgiving as the individual moves into action on the physical plane.

Words cannot properly describe the synchronous activity of spiritual consciousness as it processes thoughts and ideas and brings them forth into visible manifestation. However, by isolating the basic principles of the process—and then by incorporating them into a treatment sequence—we can approach the creative efficiency and effectiveness of the awakened ones in making our dreams a reality.

The ten principles of the manifestation process are:
1. The Principle of Attunement.
2. The Principle of Choice.
3. The Principle of Acceptance.
4. The Principle of Have.
5. The Principle of Visualization.
6. The Principle of Love.
7. The Principle of the Spoken Word.
8. The Principle of Surrender.
9. The Principle of Gratitude.
10. The Principle of Action.

We have worked with these principles in our own spiritual treatments and have taught the 10-step process in a number of seminars across the country. And based on the number of letters that we have received it is obvious that men and women below the master level of consciousness can demonstrate the fulfillment of essentially any true desire—if they choose to do so and will work with the principles on a daily basis.

Of course, we all want to move up to the level of consciousness where our good is automatically outpictured in our lives, but in the meantime we must learn how to manifest what we need today. As Elana points out in *The Superbeings*, "If an individual is experiencing a pressing need, it may be difficult at first to let go and let the grace of God come forth as the needed thing. Because our mentalities are geared to formulas and techniques, it may be propitious to follow a treatment sequence. . .until the particular desire is fulfilled."

There are an infinite number of things and experiences waiting for us in the Kingdom within, and we want to expand our consciousness to the point where we can accept all the good that God has for us. But we will not be able to enter and take over the Kingdom that has already been deeded to us—and has our name on it in the heavenly records—until we eliminate a consciousness of *need*. We can do that with the manifestation process while proving to ourselves that "we have it all and we have it now."

Isn't it time to accept our divine heritage and start living the life more abundant? The choice is ours.

CHAPTER TEN

Ten Steps to the Fulfillment of Your Desires

Step No. 1: The Principle of Attunement

This step is based on opening your heart and mind to your spiritual nature. It is tuning into that Presence and Power of God within you and recognizing that the Mind and Power of the Infinite is right where you are, individualized *as* you. I realize that this has been covered in some detail in Part I, but let's go over it again because without it you will be operating strictly on mind power; you will be engaged in a metal exercise rather than a spiritual treatment, and the result will be dramatically different.

Going back to the basics for a moment, I believe that you will agree that the Spirit of God is everywhere present, all knowing, all loving, all powerful. Now the beautiful and fascinating thing to me is that this Eternal Selfhood began to individualize Itself as me, as you, even before we came forth as distinct units of consciousness. In order for you to be, to exist, Infinite Mind had to conceive of you, and this focus of you, on you, was the beginning of the individualizing process, out of which you came into being.

As the Universal Divine Sonship contemplated Itself as you, a state of Consciousness was expressed, or pressed out. An individualized Energy Field, a force field of Consciousness, appeared. Now remember what the word "consciousness" means. It is awareness, understanding, and knowledge—and that original state of Consciousness that you had was a Superconsciousness, which means a Super-awareness, a Super-understanding, and a Super-knowledge of God.

When you are super-aware of something, when you have super-understanding of something, that "Something" literally becomes your Consciousness. The thinker and the thought become one. So in truth, the Reality of you is God knowing Itself as God, God knowing Itself as You, and You knowing yourself as God. This Trinity of Know-ingness becomes one in Consciousness, the Master Con-sciousness of the Master Self within you—which means that each one of us is a living, moving, walking, talking, rainbow-colored Energy Field of God. And within that Energy field is everything that we could possibly desire, not only for this life but for all eternity. We have the Kingdom NOW!

I hear your questions: Why am I not living a perfect life? If this pure vibration of Divine Consciousness is manifest-ing as an eternal condition of Well-being within me, how in the name of God can I ever be ill or experience disease?

If this Infinite Prosperity is individualized as me, how in the world can I possibly experience lack of supply?

If God is living *as* me now, why am I not living as God?

And the answer is. . .you have not opened the door of your thinking mind and feeling nature. That Master Self within is knocking right now, but for many of us the door is closed and all that Superconsciousness of Mastery is for naught.

How do you open the door? Let's go back to the defini-tion of consciousness. Remember that it is awareness, understanding and knowledge—and it is the key to open the door to the Secret Place. Try this experiment with me: Close your eyes and visualize a red rose. Can you see that red rose? Of course you can. You can see it in your mind's eye because it has been brought into your conscious aware-ness. You are now aware of the red rose, therefore, you are now *conscious* of it. Now think of that Master Self, the

Reality of you, around you and through you, occupying the same space that you do. To get the full impact of this awareness, you have to FEEL it, so think on this idea for a moment:

There is a Superconsciousness of God within me now. It is the Master Self that I AM in truth, the Master Consciousness that I AM. It is closer than breathing, nearer than hands and feet. I look within and sense this all-knowing Mind and I feel the Presence of Love in my heart.

Do you see what you are doing? You are becoming more aware of your True Nature, the Super Self within you. You are fanning the Divine Spark of spiritual awareness deep within your soul into a living flame of Truth. Understand that the more you are consciously aware of your God Self, the more that Self fills your consciousness. And the greater your consciousness is of this Higher Self, the greater your understanding of It will be, and the greater your understanding, the greater your knowledge—*and knowledge is power!* In the process of the expanding consciousness you literally take on the attributes of your Superconsciousness, and this is what it means to "put on Christ." You literally become that which you are conscious of.

As I have said, it is so important to spend time daily in contemplative meditation where you ponder and reflect upon, and think about, and consider fully the wholeness and completeness of the Master Self that you are—knowing that through that contemplation you are drawing the Presence of God right into your consciousness. With this infilling your consciousness becomes Cause to your world. You are no longer just an effect. With Christ in you, your hope of glory, you become Cause—and truly, all things are then possible.

Step No. 2: The Principle of Choice

I wrote in *The Superbeings* that you should focus your thoughts on what you really want in life. In other words, before you reach the level of consciousness where the

Choices of Self are automatically outpictured, you must assume the authority to choose the things, circumstances, situations, or experiences that you deeply desire, knowing that "desire" is the first step in the action cycle. Without desire nothing happens. Without desire the universe and Planet Earth would not have been created. Without desire you would not exist.

Where do desires come from? Unselfish, good-for-all desires come forth as an activity of your Higher Self, stirring you to realize that It wants to do more for you, through you. When your aspiration is for something that cannot hurt you or anyone else, and will bring good into your life and the lives of others, it is your spiritual Self tugging at your heart's door trying to get your attention.

As Emmet Fox has said, "Get the thought of what you want as clear as you can. If you say 'I want something, I don't know what—I will leave it to God'; if you say 'I want a business, it may be a farm or a shop—I will leave it to Divine Mind', you are foolish. What are you here for? You must have some desires and wishes, because you represent God here."[1]

So make a list of what you want and put it in writing, and understand what you are doing in this choosing process. You are taking a close look at your life and finding all the soft spots, all the empty spaces, all the imperfections—you are determining what it is that will make your life totally fulfilled at this time. By choosing what you really want and knowing that you have the power to bring it into manifestation, and then by doing so, you are cooperating with Self in revealing the ever-present Reality.

Once you begin to exercise dominion by choosing, the Spirit within you will speak to you through your intuition, guiding you to choose even greater experiences or showing you something better from the vantage point of the higher vision. But you must make the first move. You must make the choice and then follow the manifestation process all the way through the action step as though your path was illuminated by the wisdom of Spirit every inch of the way. If you begin the process by tuning into your Higher Consciousness you will find it difficult to make mistakes or take the wrong turn—*even if the choice you made was not in your best interest*. You see, once you make a choice as God's expression, and stay in tune with that Master Vibration within, Spirit will literally go before you to straighten out the crooked places in the road and will keep you on safe ground.

A friend of mine once made the decision to apply for a particular job that he knew could be his based on his experience and qualifications. So in the manifestation process he chose that specific job and was quickly moving toward realization of his desire when Spirit stepped in and revealed a completely different career opportunity offering more money and greater fulfillment. But you see, he didn't just sit around waiting for something to happen. He made a choice, and through the activity of that decision-making, brought himself into alignment with the higher vision of his God-Self. So don't be afraid to choose, or to make a decision. Decide what you want and go after it!

Many people also get confused about the choosing process, thinking that if God has already given them everything—if they are already complete and whole—why do they have to choose. The answer is that all the good that God has for us has already been given to the Reality within, our Higher Self. In truth, we do have everything right now, but we have to claim it. In essence, we are choosing the *spiritual* equivalent for that which we desire in physical form, and when we choose it, the spiritual equivalent moves into the manifestation chamber where it becomes the *mental* equivalent of the physical form or experiences. Everything is stepped down from the spiritual plane to the mental plane, and then proceeds out into the physical world to appear in material form.

Step No. 3: The Principle of Acceptance

Simply stated, this step means that you cannot have the fulfillment of your desires without acceptance. When you choose something, the spiritual equivalent will move into the subjective area of mind, but unless you accept it right then, it will leave and return to the higher realms of consciousness. A spiritual equivalent does not stay where it is not welcomed and accepted.

Charles Fillmore explained that all of God's gifts to us are first in thought form, and when we appropriate and accept these thought forms, a pattern or expression of that thought form is established in consciousness. He says, "The patterns arrest or 'bottle up' the free electric units that sustain the visible thing."[2]

From the writings of Ernest Holmes we see that "Spirit cannot make the gift unless you accept it. Life may have given everything to you, but only that which you accept is yours to use."[3]

So you accept the increased income, the new job, the new car, the new home, the new relationship. Once you choose what you want you accept the thing or experience mentally and with the fullness of your feeling nature. And as pointed out by another friend, you must also be prepared to accept your good physically. She explains:

"I affirmed, visualized, meditated, prayed and affirmed again on a financial dilemma that I was about to face. I accepted mentally and spiritually that the money would be there in plenty of time in God's wonderful way. I KNEW it would come, but when it did, it came in such an unusual way that believe it or not, I turned it down! I knew the very second I said 'no' that I had made a large mistake. Talk about throwing a monkey wrench in the whole deal! A tough lesson—and one I won't forget."

Step No. 4: The Principle of Have

When you accept something, you HAVE it—even if what you accept is still in invisible form. If you have a need and Spirit gives you the fulfillment of that need—and you accept—your consciousness will begin to shift from a sense of need to a sense of HAVE. The fulfillment is yours even before you see it in visible form or experience. And when you have something as a part of your consciousness you can "I AM" it with affirmative statements and thoughts.

For example, if you choose and accept an all-sufficiency of supply, the pattern of that divine idea is established in mind. Therefore, in truth, you HAVE the abundant supply, and you make it a reality in consciousness by personalizing it:

I am rich! I am the lavish abundance of the universe individualized. All that the Father has is mine and my prosperity is assured. I am now filled and thrilled with the consciousness of abundance and plenty.

Do you see now that an affirmation at this step in the process becomes an *acknowledgement*? You are simply stating that which is absolutely true, rather than trying to convince the subconscious of something that you hope will be true at some future date. By working with the principle of HAVE, you are working in the NOW, where the activity of God always is.

As Joel Goldsmith has written—"By acknowledging that we *have*, we shall demonstrate *have*."[4] That is why this step is so important in moving us away from the sense of need, because a consciousness of need simply produces more need. Affirming out of a consciousness of need is like pouring water in a bucket with a hole in the bottom.

Step No. 5: The Principle of Visualization

When you use the imaging powers of your mind you are working as Self works; through the power of creative visualization you are in the closest proximity to the activity of God-Mind. Remember that *energy follows thought*, and it is through controlled imagination that unconditioned energy is conditioned into thoughtforms which produce the effects on the physical level. You create form out of thought substance through your power to visualize, either by sharp and distinctive mental pictures or by sensing and feeling the image of fulfillment and completion in your mind.

In the manifestation process I use the word "visualization" more often that imagination because I am talking about *controlled* mental picturing. To some people imagination is like day-dreaming, and while that activity does have its place it does not have the power and thrust of vivid mental images that have been scripted, produced and directed in your mind with you in the starring role. With this kind of disciplined mental production you can truly mold conditions and shape events.

When you visualize, or practice controlled imagery, be sure to experience the fulfillment of your desires in the present moment; always work in the NOW. And instead of "seeing yourself" on the stage of life having, being and doing according to your heart's desire, you must *be* that person. Seeing another face and form that looks like you enjoying health and wholeness does not have the power to properly condition the energy. You must combine your conscious awareness with the form and experience and *feel* the perfection throughout your being; you must *live* the prosperity, the ideal relationship, the true place success in your mind as the one personally enjoying the manifest good.

Capture the view of "the happy ending"—the finished episode. For example, if you want a new car, experience your conscious mind, feeling nature and physical body as having, driving and enjoying that car, constantly remembering that it is yours NOW. Do not imagine yourself sitting across from a banker trying to arrange financing—jump across time to the end result.

And be sure to add color, dimension and sound to your mental movie. See the beauty of your imaged environment; watch the movement of people and bring in life and dimension to their activities; listen as your friends congratulate you on your radiant health or your new success and prosperity. Someone once told me, "What you see is what you get"—so create a masterpiece for yourself—not outlining how your good is to come to you or how your desires are going to be fulfilled. That is none of your business. Just know that what you are seeing in mind, Spirit will create in form and experience "in perfect ways for the good of all."

One way that I have found to sharpen my practice of creative visualization is to write out the complete and finished scenario, just as I would like to see it on the screen of my mind. And as I read these words the images take shape and I see and hear and feel the total fulfillment of my desires.

Another point: Every scene, every picture, every character, and every situation in your mental play must be totally positive. Do not allow one single negative aspect to enter your mind during the process. Always see the best. Always image from your highest vision.

Step No. 6: The Principle of Love

While you are visualizing your good be sure to *love* what you see. Pour all the love you have into those finished pictures—generate that warm, passionate and powerful feeling of love and let it radiate through those images in your mind. Remember that Love Energy is the most powerful force in the universe, the power behind the whole thrust of creation, and that Love Power will clothe your images with radiant substance for perfect manifestation in the physical world.

Substance is the creative energy of everything visible, the divine idea underlying all physical manifestation. When you consciously radiate the energy of love, when with purpose of mind you send forth currents of love through your mental pictures, when you love what you see with deep-deep feeling, you are propelling the substance and giving it a clear path to follow as it moves from cause into effect. Substance is the raw material out of which everything visible is formed, and love is the animating force that forms it.

When you love what you see with all your heart, your mental images will stand out with great clarity and will become *real* (substantial) to you. Through the love vibration you unite the conscious, subconscious and Superconscious phases of your mind, and you truly embody the pattern that represents the fulfillment of your desires. Love power will help you to realize the truth of that which you are seeking—and this realization must, by law, outpicture itself in your world. As above, so below. As within, so without.

Step No. 7: The Principle of the Spoken Word

God made individual being, male and female, by the power of the Word, and each one of us is a co-creator with God using that same power. As Jehovah said to Job, "Thou shalt also decree a thing, and it shall be established unto thee." Most of us do not realize the power of the spoken word but it is spelled out very clearly in Proverbs 18:21— "Death and life are in the power of the tongue." Every word you speak causes a vibration in the universal energy field, and the effect of that vibration returns to you in direct response to the nature of the word. It is impossible for your words to return unto you void.

Matthew 12:37 states it this way: "By your words you will be justified, and by your words you will be condemned." The words that you want justified (proved right) in the manifestation process are the spoken words of faith that acknowledge that action of Spirit. It is the *closure* to your active part in the treatment sequence. Through your words, addressed to *you*—the only consciousness that could possibly restrict your good—you *let* the manifestation take place and you firmly declare that IT IS DONE! It is knowing that you have faithfully done your part, and you are calling on your energy of faith to stand guard at the door of consciousness and to keep that door open for the outpouring of substance on wings of love.

When the faith faculty is called into action through the use of the spoken word, it becomes the foundation of your belief system. It takes your words "IT IS DONE" and responds triumphantly "AND IT IS SO!" And remember that the activity of the faith center causes a chain reaction in the other power centers on the subconscious level to give you even greater authority to shape events and create new experiences in your life.

Step No. 8: The Principle of Surrender

In this step you let go and let Spirit do its perfect work in bringing forth the fulfillment of your desires. It means that you are totally willing to accept the Way and the Truth of your Divine Consciousness, which is always so much more than you could possible conceive. God's Will is *Good Will*, and as that Will is made manifest in your life you will see that Spirit wants more for you than you want for yourself—more supply than you have asked for; more joy, peace and beauty; a perfect body rather than just relief from pain and sickness; an ideal relationship instead of one that will soon fade away. When you surrender to God you are surrendering to a greater good and a higher degree of happiness than you have ever known.

At this step in the process you release your desires, the visualized scenario, your willfulness, your entire consciousness. You turn everything over to the Master Consciousness within and let each and every detail of your life be perfected by the Divine Vision, Power and Action. You get out of the way of the Divine Circuits and let God be God. And how will you know if you have truly surrendered? By the total lack of concern, anxiety, and outside pressure in consciousness. This negative energy will have been replaced with the positive vibrations of peace, joy and confidence, and you will find yourself beginning to live in a state of grace.

One day I was meditating on the idea of grace, and the thoughts that came forth from within said that the first seven steps of the manifestation process are simply the momentum steps—much like building pressure in a boiler—that these steps were necessary to develop thrust to move us from a third dimensional vibration up to the fourth dimensional frequency. I was told that it was much like an airplane picking up speed and gathering power as it rolls down the runway for a take-off, and that when we let go and let God, we are actually moving into the consciousness of grace.

Now there are two ways of "letting go and letting God." One way is to turn everything over to Spirit while maintaining the same state of consciousness that produced the problem in the first place. This is like saying, "Prosper me, heal me, but you've got to do it without my help." It does not work that way, but it does work when you let go and let God work *through* your uplifted thinking and feeling natures. It does work when you surrender to Spirit after you have done your part in raising consciousness. That is when you begin to live under grace, the love of God in action where cosmic law works on a higher frequency to dissolve the negative appearances and make all things new.

Step No. 9: The Principle of Gratitude

This step represents a joyful heart filled with praise and thanksgiving, an overwhelming feeling of gratitude because you KNOW that your problems are solved and your needs are met. Always remember that your desires are first fulfilled in consciousness, and then they come forth in the outer world clothed with materiality—so the secret of this step is to be thankful while your good is still invisible! You cannot wait until you possess the visible form to express your gratitude or you will delay the entire process, or cancel it out altogether.

Once you have surrendered to the Good Will of God in Step 8 everything is "GO" from that moment on. The universal creative system is in operation and the activity of Spirit is moving in divine order. But for you to be in tune with *all* the channels that Spirit has selected for your good there must be a deep feeling of gratitude in your heart. Gratitude releases a dynamic current of spiritual energy to go before you to exert a mighty influence in your world. It not only eliminates negative patterns in the subconscious caused by ingratitude, it also forms a connecting link—a bridge—between you and every possible source of good in your life. Of course, there is only one Source, but Divine Mind works in mysterious ways to perform magnificent wonders through an infinite number of channels. And through a feeling of gratitude and praise for the Master Consciousness within, you put yourself in alignment with all of the riches of the universe.

Now tell me. . .have you ever seen anyone with a grateful heart lack for any good thing?

Step No. 10: The Principle of Action

After you complete your spiritual treatment you must move into action. If you just sit around waiting for God to drop your good in your lap you will be shown scores of new ways to sit, because the Law works through you according to your activity in the NOW.

This realization came to me several years ago. Jan and I had fallen into the metaphysical trap that says "turn away from this world and let your uplifted spiritual consciousness outpicture itself." That's fine if you are working from a spiritual consciousness—and that is the pitfall because most of us do not know where we are in consciousness. So while we are doing our spiritual work we must also use good common sense. We rise from our prayers, meditations and spiritual treatments and follow through with the action that is intuitively indicated to us; we make a definite move which the Masters call the positioning process. We position ourselves through action in order to receive our good.

When you complete your spiritual treatment move out into the world to do that which is before you to do to the very best of your ability, always listening to that inner feeling for guidance. If you are out of work, take the first thing that comes to you while continuing to work spiritually for your True Place. If you are out of money, find a way to earn some, and do the best you can—even if it is sweeping floors—while you are working on a prosperity consciousness.

Remember that God always meets you on the level where you are in consciousness, which means that regardless of where you are in your spiritual development, God can and will meet your needs. But you have your part to play as a co-creator. And the greater the sense of separation from the Spirit of God within, the greater the activity on the physical plane must be—with each action dedicated to honoring your God-Self.

For example, if you are still filled with fear and doubt, even after your spiritual treatment, then get as active as you can and as quickly as you can. Begin to clean the house (or yard, car or office) as it has never been cleaned before—or complete that project that you have been putting off and do it to the very best of your ability. Once you have completed this initial work, turn within and ask your Higher Self, "What would you like for me to do now?" The thought will flash into your mind and you must follow through to the letter.

Through these activities and the expenditure of physical energy you will find burdens dropping from your shoulders and a sense of peace entering your consciousness. Through your actions you will not only eliminate your fears but also the cause of your fears. When this happens your intuitive faculty will open again and the hunches, the inner feelings and the guidance will come forth to lead you in the direction that God wants you to go. And follow each lead, thinking of each one as a vital link in a chain reaction that will result in the fulfillment of your desires.

Step out into action today and do what needs to be done, and soon you will find Spirit working through you to perform all that is appointed for you to do. You will then live your life as a beholder of God in action, and your Earth will truly be your Heaven.

CHAPTER ELEVEN

Applying the Steps in Sequence: A Meditative Treatment

In the spiritual treatment of the manifestation process please keep in mind that the secret of success is in the sequence, because each step sets the stage in consciousness for the one that follows. You tune into the Presence within and take on the spiritual vibration. You choose that which is your heart's desire, knowing that the reason you have this desire is because Spirit is wanting it through you—so you are choosing that which your Master Self has already chosen for you. And then you accept the gift, and by accepting it mentally and emotionally you *have* it, and the mental equivalent for it is formed in consciousness.

By seeing it in visible form and experience through creative visualization you are clearing the channels of any opposing views and are molding the unconditioned energy according to the clarity of your vision. By loving what you see you are focusing the flow of substance through your consciousness, and by speaking the word that it is done you are taking an act of faith that acknowledges the action of Spirit.

At this point you feel the mighty currents working in and through you, and you surrender everything to the Master Consciousness and get the lower nature completely out of the way. Now the Energy of God flows through a consciousness of like vibration. With deep feeling you express your gratitude and move forward with a powerful feeling of poise and confidence as you take the appropriate action in your world.

Through this particular spiritual treatment you are duplicating the automatic activity of Cosmic Consciousness in a step-by-step process, and as you learn to manifest the fulfillment of your desires and become more proficient with the treatment, you will find that your consciousness will expand to where the entire process is accomplished independently of your thinking. And this is what it means to "take no thought."

The Spiritual Treatment

Sit up straight in a comfortable chair and relax completely. Take several deep breaths to clear your mind and let go of all pressing thoughts and concerns. Be aware of your breathing and breathe in peace and breathe out tension. Breathe in white light and breathe out all misqualified energy, remembering that energy follows thought.

Now with your mind and feeling nature, begin to sense and feel the Presence of God that is all around you and within you. Contemplate this Body of Light, this all-knowing Mind, this Heart of infinite Love that occupies the same space that you do. Let this joyful Spirit fill your consciousness with Itself and feel the dynamic Power as your mental and emotional natures begin to pulsate to that spiritual vibration. You are now aware of your God-Self. Let that Master Self speak to you now. . .

I will never leave you nor forsake you. I am with you always, for you are my expression, the light of my Light. I have fulfilled Myself as you and have given Myself to you. All that I am, you are, for you are my expression.

I am all that you can conceive of me to be—your supply, your health, your work, your relationships, your protection, your all. I ask only that you abide in me and look to me as your all-sufficiency, knowing that I withhold nothing from you. Now choose that which you desire in my name, the name of I AM.

Say to yourself silently:

I am God in expression. God is as me now, and the True Self of me has assumed Its rightful position on the throne of my heart, for the feeling of love tells me so. I now have the power of dominion. I am now a co-creator with God. I now have divine authority to manifest the fulfillment of my desires, and I use this power rightly and wisely.

In your mind see a white screen, and on this screen see the words "I choose"—with lines following as if on a ruled tablet. Now fill in the blank spaces in your own handwriting. Simply imagine that you are writing on the inner tablet of mind the choices for this particular time in your life. After you have mentally written your desires, go back and focus on each word with great clarity. See the meaning of the words, and let them become deeply impressed in your mind.

Now say to yourself silently:

I accept the fulfillment of this desire now. With all my mind, with all my heart, with all my soul, I accept this fulfillment now. And I *feel* the spiritual idea representing this fulfillment entering my consciousness. It is the idea of completion, and it has moved into my feeling nature. Its vibration is warm and pleasant, and I love the feeling. I accept *all* the good that God has for me now.

Because I have accepted the fulfillment of my desire, I now *have* it. I now have the object of my desire. I no longer need what I formerly desired because I now have it! And it feels so good. Through this knowledge of *have*, I know that I AM that which I desire. I AM abundance! I AM radiant wholeness! I AM the ideal relationship! I AM the total fulfillment of every desire!

In your mind's eye look at the white screen again, and on the screen begin to play your mental movie. Take yourself into the carefully constructed scenario and in your mind begin doing, being, having, and enjoying your good in overflowing measure. Play the joyful, happy, and freedom-loving role with all the enthusiasm you can muster. Add color, sound, and dimension. Etch every detail deeply in consciousness, knowing that what you are *being, doing,* and *having* in your imagination is NOW—the present time—and not at a point in the future. In your controlled imagery, be and do and have the best that you can conceive. Lift up your vision and image the highest and most fulfilling scenes that you can produce in your mind. Feel the excitement of seeing your desire already fulfilled. It is so wonderful! See it! Feel it! Know it!

With your mind focused on those beautiful images, begin now to let all the love you can feel in your heart pour out. *Love* those images of fulfillment! Say to yourself:

Oh how I love what I see. I love the joyous expressions and the happy scenes. I love doing what I love to do. I love being what I want to be. I love having what I want to have. I love the pictures of total fulfillment that I am now seeing in my mind and feeling in my heart.

After several minutes of visioning your fulfillment, close the curtain on the screen of your mind and turn within to the ever-present Reality of You—your Master Self—letting the feeling of that Presence enter your heart. Say to yourself, aloud if possible:

Nothing is too good for me to have or experience, so in the name and through the power of my Holy Self I speak the word. I let there be total fulfillment now! I let *all* the good that God has for me come forth into manifestation here and now. I let the Spirit of God work in and through me to meet every need, solve every problem, and appear as the fulfillment of every desire. My faith in the loving givingness of God is mighty, and my good does now come forth into visible form and experience. My All Good does now come forth by the power of my word. It is done. And it is so!

And silently:

I now totally and completely surrender to the activity of God, the only power at work in my life. I let go and let God be God. I let go and let the Spirit of God do Its perfect work in and through me.

My Holy Master Self within, the fathering and mothering aspects of my being, I completely surrender now to your Good Will. I know that even in my highest vision I cannot behold the fullness of the glory that You have planned for me since the beginning. So I release my needs, desires, images, and will to You, and I am willing to accept my highest and greatest good now. I know that by releasing everything to You, I have released the mighty currents of Creative Energy into my life and affairs. And I know that only that which is good, beautiful, abundant, peaceful, and joyful is now flowing into perfect manifestation in my world.

Thank You, my Beloved Sacredness, for this new life of love and light. Thank You for total fulfillment now. My heart overflows with gratitude and joy. My cup runneth over and I am so thankful. Praise God! Praise God! Praise God!

Rest for a period in the silence.

I now move into action in my world as a co-creator with God, always listening to the inner Guide and doing that which is mine to do to the very best of my ability.

NOTE: There is another application of this ten-step program where the process is turned totally inward as a method of consciousness conditioning. A 2-cassette tape album by the Prices titled "The Hidden Splendor"—recorded live during a 1991 workshop—discusses this inner manifestation process in detail. It is available from The Quartus Foundation, P.O. Box 1768, Boerne, Texas 78006.

CHAPTER TWELVE

Questions and Answers about the Manifestation Process

1. *Should I include more than one desire at a time in using the spiritual treatment?*

Answer: Only if the fulfillment as seen during the visualization stage can easily incorporate a number of choices. For example, if you are working for increased income, a new home and a new automobile, these particular desires can be seen with great clarity in your visioning because of their association. However, if you are treating to harmonize a relationship—in addition to manifesting a financial all-sufficiency—you should follow the process for each one independently. Another point to consider: how many desires or choices can you comfortably work with at one time?

2. *Should I treat each day for the same desire?*

Answer: Once you have completed the manifestation process with great feeling, you have done your part—and the only reason to go back and treat again for the same thing would be if you had a downward shift in consciousness regarding the fulfillment of that particular desire. When this happens, it means that a link in the manifestation chain has broken, and your job is to repair it. To do this, sit quietly and backtrack from Step No. 10, going back through each step until you pick up a negative feeling or vibration in your solar plexus. This is telling you that some adjustment will be necessary at this stage in the process. For instance, let's say that you treated on Monday for increased income, and when you completed the sequence you were totally assured that the money would appear. But by Thursday you began to feel a sense of anxiety, showing you that there was a gap in the circuit. The moment this uneasiness appears, go to a quiet place and ask yourself:

• Have I taken appropriate action based on what I intuitively feel that I should do?

• Have I continually expressed a deep feeling of joy and gratitude?

• Have I truly surrendered everything to Spirit?

• Can I say "It is done!" with great faith?

• Have I maintained a feeling of intense love in seeing the fulfillment of my desires?

• Was there great clarity in my mental pictures? Did I really *see* and *feel* the fulfillment of my desires?

• Do I feel that I *have* my good right now, even though it is not yet visible?

• Have I accepted my good with all of my mind and heart?

You go back only as far as Step No. 2, because once you choose it is not necessary to repeat this step. The only exception might be if you were hesitant and inhibited in choosing during the initial treatment, in which case you should repeat the entire process again. In most situations, however, you will feel a "dip" somewhere along the line of steps 10 back to 3, and that is where you should start again with the treatment. Never let one day pass without going through the appropriate steps if you feel even the slightest drop in consciousness.

In one particular instance, Jan and I had only to go back to Step No. 9 to spot the problem. For some reason we had not completely stirred up that feeling of joyful gratitude, so we began right at this step and did what was necessary to open our hearts to an attitude of thanksgiving. To "prime the pump" Jan took pots and pans and wooden spoons from the kitchen and insisted that we have a parade through the house singing songs of joyful praise to the

Lord. I thought that she had lost her mind but played along anyway, and within a minute or two we both were giggling and having a marvelous time. We became as little children and let the laughter shake the walls as the joy energy began to flow. Soon the gratitude filled our hearts and within a short time we had our demonstration.

3. *What if I don't know what to put at the top of my desire list? I have so many priorities?*

Answer: You will quickly learn how to be so efficient with the manifestation process that you will literally be looking for new choices to add to your list. But start with what you consider to be your major heart's desire. In many cases people have told us that when they came to the choosing stage and began to write their choices on the tablet in their minds, "something" within would erase one goal and substitute another. Or as one woman told us, "I had a list of five goals, which I wrote on the screen of my mind. As I was focusing on each one of them, number five suddenly moved up and changed places with number one." This shows us that Spirit will work with us in the choosing process, but we begin the list with what we consider our top priority.

4. *Should the manifestation process replace my regular meditations?*

Answer: No. Through daily meditations you will eventually move into the natural order process where the manifestation of your good is automatic.

5. *What if I cannot clearly see the fulfillment of my desires during the visualization stage?*

Answer: First examine to see if your choices are clear and readily adaptable to the imaging process. Many people cannot "see" fulfillment because their choices are too vague. Next, practice the visualization step just as you would practice anything else to develop proficiency. Start by focusing on a picture or outside scene, then close your eyes and duplicate that image in your mind. The more you work with this soul faculty the clearer your images will be, and the greater the clarity, the greater the power of manifestation.

If you continue to have difficulty with mental imaging, then work with *feeling* the fulfillment you desire. Become aware of the new home, for example, by entertaining the idea of the home and all that it represents to you. Let your appreciation of it impress you, and *feel* the victory of accomplishment. And keep practicing until the feeling is totally natural to you.

6. What is the normal timeframe for the manifestation?

Answer: It truly depends on where you are on the spiral of consciousness. However, from studying actual case histories I can say that a seemingly large number of demonstrations occur within a period of 21 days. So much is also dependent on the strength of the desire, and to what extent the faith faculty has been awakened. I also feel that the clarity of the vision (or the depth of the feeling) has much to do with timing. Clear and sharp mental pictures, or strong powerful intuitive feelings accented with great love, will definitely speed up the process.

7. Is there any particular action that I can take in Step No. 10 that will help me to rise in consciousness?

Answer: An awakened one once told me—"Choose what you want and then give the equivalent of it away." He said that this was action of the highest order to overcome time and expand consciousness. Here are six examples of that philosophy.

• Do you desire love? Give more love to all and it shall be returned to you, not only universally, but from those whose love you treasure most.

• Do you desire more time to accomplish more? Then give more time to spiritual matters and all the clocks in the world will stop so that you will have the time you need for other activities.

• Do you desire more energy and vitality? Then begin each day by stirring up the gift of joy, and joyfully radiate the Light of God within to encompass this planet. This Light Energy propelled by joy will return to you in steady streams of vitality throughout the day.

• Do you desire more money? Then give more of what you have for the benefit of others, and it will be returned to you in overflowing measure.

• Do you desire more wisdom? Then counsel with those who need your encouragement, according to your present level of understanding, and your path will be illumined with the Wisdom of Spirit.

• Do you desire greater health? Then see every individual only as the perfect Being of God, recognizing nothing but radiant wholeness in every person regardless of appearances. Through this highest vision you will be seeing *yourself*, and your body will respond accordingly.

Give more of yourself and gain God in the exchange. The secret of mastery is truly in the giving.

Being Spiritually Rich and Materially Happy

Introduction to
Part III

In this particular section of the book the objective is to expand our consciousness of the *Truth* of our unlimited Abundance. We want to be so clear that the manifestation of supply is automatic in our lives—so that we never again live under the cloud of insufficiency. To do this we must first recognize the fact that "I of myself can do nothing"—yet *I* of my Self can do all things! It is the transferring of the financial government from the ego of the lower nature to the indwelling High Fiscal Master Who is superbly capable of radiating and attracting a continuous all-sufficiency of legal tender.

And remember that we do not have to *create* anything. Oh, I know that there is much talk in metaphysical circles about "creating your own reality." But if you have read and studied the chapters in this book in the sequence presented, you know that Reality already exists, and that our role is simply to let it be revealed through us. The conscious mind must look beyond itself and see with the inner eye the Vast Reservoir of Mind where all is complete as the Finished Kingdom. We must recognize that the personality is not the Giver, Doer, Supplier, Adjuster or Healer, rather, it is the *receiver* of the Divine Energies from the Living Reservoir and the channel through which those gifts flow. We must understand that "what the mind can conceive, the *Self* can achieve." To claim our good is to accept the fullness of our Estate. To visualize our good is to see through the High Vision of the Master within and behold the infinite abundance that is already ours. To speak the word is to decree the Truth of Being that is eternally expressed in the omnipotent name of I AM. Our mental treatments should be raised up to the level of Spiritual Therapy to dissolve the resistance that is holding back the natural flow of our good. Our I AM affirmations are to be declarations of the Truth of Self addressed to that Self, with our meditations focused on reaching into the Supernatural Light within, becoming One with the Light, and living as the Light.

Each one of us has lived as the prodigal son, and even now we may be at that mid-point between arising from the pig pen and the moment of the Father's full embrace. Jesus tells us nothing in Luke 15:11 about the interim period between the time that the son came to himself and later when the father saw him at a distance—yet esoterically this is the Wilderness Experience. It is a time of confusion and uncertainty when every suppressed emotion flies up to tear us down. It is the breaking away from the human sense of being and making the firm decision to tread the spiritual path, which drives the ego into a frenzy—yet we know that the spiritual life is the only worthwhile choice. But we wonder about the *practicality* of it; just how can we live "spiritually" when everything in the material world seems to be falling apart? For a time we may even try to fix the effects projected on the outer screen, but finally we come to the point where we recognize the total insanity of living in this barren land—in this "far country"—and we say "enough of this!" And with this change of attitude we begin our rise in consciousness to seek and find the Truth of our Lavish Inheritance—knowing that with every degree of realized Truth comes a greater outpouring and fulfilling of the desires and needs experienced in consciousness—as symbolized by the best robe, the ring, the shoes, the feast, and the merry-making.

During this journey toward the Light of Truth we drop

all thought of doing, being, and having anything from the level of ego. We move beyond "the Wilderness" in consciousness—out of the mental-emotional wasteland that tells us we need to be prospered, healed, or fixed—and into the joyous light of knowing that we have *never* been impoverished, sick, or broken. As our consciousness shifts to this higher level we understand that as Spiritual Beings, we truly do have everything now. It is not the ego that recognizes this fullness of life, however. It is that awakening part of our personality where the light dawns and we become aware that the Master I AM *is* everything, *has* everything, and is *doing* everything now through our awareness.

Let's look at these additional points for greater understanding:

1. Money is not supply; it is the symbol of supply. Supply is the creative/creating Energy radiating from our Divine Consciousness, the I AM Presence.

2. This radiation from the Source within is the Law of Abundance, the Principle of Prosperity. Our conscious awareness of this Law and Principle becomes the channel through which the radiation takes place.

3. The radiating Energy appears as visible supply (money) as Cause moves into effect through consciousness. The trend of our thoughts and feelings can either restrict or release the natural flow of this Energy.

4. Even though we may perceive ourselves as a physical body with a mind that thinks and emotions that feel, we must transfer our identification to the spiritual realm and constantly remind ourselves that we are Spiritual Beings— pure Spiritual Consciousness.

5. As Spiritual Beings we must be aware that we have no needs, yet we can look "below" and see that the unrealized consciousness perceives need. We let those needs be fulfilled by maintaining our Divine Identity and beholding the mighty Rays of Spirit moving through our consciousness to "make all things new."

6. We function on Earth as a Trinity—God in Three Persons—as the Infinite Mind of Self, as the conscious awareness of the activity of Self, and as the Spiritual Ener-

gy flowing through that Awareness.

We have left the far country and we are on the journey home, and it will not be long until we feel the embrace and the kiss of the Holy One within. At that moment the infusion of Spirit transforms the personality and the little "i" no longer exists. We then have "that mind" that was in Christ Jesus, and all power and authority is returned.

Until that Magic Moment let's remember that it is the Divine Self and not the personality Who "opens the windows of heaven"—Who "opens unto thee his good treasure"—Who "has pleasure in the prosperity of his servant"—and Who "giveth thee power to get wealth" by showing us its eternal reality.

Through our consciousness of this magnificent activity of the Master Self, our lives overflow with spiritual riches and material happiness. What a way to live!

CHAPTER THIRTEEN

A Consciousness of Abundance

In my book, *The Planetary Commission*[1], I wrote that "We must understand the principles of supply so that we are not affected by anything that happens to the economic system." What is the economic system? Rather than describing it as "free enterprise" and discussing monetary standards, supply and demand, etc., let's look at it in terms of consciousness.

Everything that happens in the physical world is an effect of consciousness, individual and collective. Accordingly, the availability of money to purchase goods and services and fulfill needs is directly related to the mental, emotional and spiritual vibrations of each man and woman—and the race as a whole. From this aspect, the world's economic system can be viewed as *"the international economy of consciousness."* And this is where we are finding the trouble spots. Material well-being, monetary resources and productive power are being weakened through a consciousness of burden and loss in the race mind, which is affecting people, organizations, institutions and governments.

Perhaps the solution to the problem is to go back to that statement from the book and rephrase it this way: "We must understand the many principles of supply and the process of manifestation so that we will not be vulnerable to the economic depression of humanity's collective consciousness." This means that we will work in *consciousness*, with action following on the third-dimensional plane as we recognize Cause sending forth Its mighty Rays through us to appear as form and experience. Accordingly, our first step in expanding our consciousness of abundance is to address the question of spirit and matter.

Removing the "versus" between spirituality and materiality.

The word "versus" means "in contest against"—which really does not make sense in this situation because there is no conflict between the two. Where we do find a battle is between spiritual values and *materialism*. Materialism is accompanied by greed, hate, and aggression, the antithesis of a spiritual life, and because of this, matter and materiality have ben given a bad rap. But if we are going to live in the material world (even though we are not of it), we had better watch our condemnations and denials because that which we deny we lose.

An ancient esoteric truth spells it out for us: "Matter is spirit at its lowest point of manifestation and spirit is matter at its highest." And our work is to learn how to balance the absolute with the relative and see the unity of substance and form. In the energy of life and the forces of matter there is only oneness, and we must understand this if we are to master the science of manifestation.

Remember that energy is real and matter is energy, therefore matter is real. Every visible thing is an expression of consciousness, and that includes money, which means that money is spiritual. Can you look at money in that light? Can you see it as energy in manifestation, as a unity of substance and form, as life appearing as matter? If there are any mental/emotional blips that say "no" or "maybe," then this is an area that you may need to work on until your consciousness is clear. Just remember that matter is spirit at its lowest point of manifestation and that there is nothing in all the universe that is not spiritually material and materially spiritual.

At this point I want to relieve a burden in consciousness for those of you who are dedicated to the spiritual life and are experiencing an insufficiency of money. Hear this: A limited supply of money does not necessarily mean that you have failed in your efforts to follow the spiritual path. It simply means that you are not using the proper spiritual dynamics. The Ageless Wisdom texts are filled with cases of advanced spiritual Lights who were baffled by the mystery of mastering money, and the early Christian Mystics called it the greatest of all the struggles of the spiritual aspirants and devoted disciples.

The reasons for this seeming scarcity are two-fold. First, the attitude of the collective consciousness toward that which was used as a medium of exchange—an attitude brought about by humanity's critical needs. When the needs were not met, the individual's feeling nature was knifed with fear, which led to grasping, greed, jealousy, and hate. Because these attitudes were so prevalent among the masses, the collective consciousness became totally unbalanced regarding supply, which even today is outpic- turing as disastrous economic conditions in the world.

The second reason for insufficiency among aspirants is that they do not view the physical world as spiritual, thus there is no connection in consciousness between the ideas of substance and form. Perhaps you can identify with this way of thinking. You have sought and found the Kingdom within and discovered that "all things" have indeed been given you, yet you seem to have difficulty releasing the "things" into manifestation. To find the reason why let's go back to the Trinity, a concept that Christianity borrowed from Ancient Wisdom.

In the Christian Trinity we have the Father, the Son, and the Holy Spirit. The Father symbolizes Will and Power, the Infinite *IS*. The Son is the Christ Aspect, the *Self*, eternal Love and Wisdom embodying the fullness of the Godhead as Infinite Being—remaining forever in the Absolute. The Holy Spirit is *Active Intelligence and Inspiration*—the Creative Energy flowing from the Individualized Presence of God and working through the consciousness of the individual. Now here is the key: The Ancients taught that the indwelling Christ or High Self does not "create" on the lower planes of manifestation. Rather, It sends forth Its Cosmic Rays (Holy Spirit) as the creator—yet many mystics and metaphysicians today attempt to live in the Absoluteness of God without being consciously aware of the *Activity* of God, the Divine Action that transforms the invisible into the visible.

Recall that it is the indwelling Presence Who opens the windows of heaven, Who provides the power, and Who makes all grace (the Divine Influence) abound toward us. In other words, the Master within sends forth the very Thought Energy of its Infinite Mind—the Spirit of the Lord—as the manifesting Agent. Think of the sun. It does not come into direct bodily contact with the Earth. If it did, our planet would cease to exist. The sun performs its cosmic function by sending forth its rays as light, as warmth, as power, as radiant energy—and this "Shining" corresponds to the Third Aspect of Divinity, the Creative Force.

This Third Aspect is also known as the God of Manifestation, so we are beginning to understand that if we are going to be channels for the Divine Expression we must be aware of the working Power of God; we cannot remain totally in the Absolute. Yes, we continue our meditations on the Christ within because it is through the awareness of the Self that the creative energy flows. We continue our attunement with the Absolute while recognizing and feeling the activity of Spirit through us. By working as an instrument for that activity, we are cooperating in an active partnership with all Aspects of our Divinity.

How do we establish this partnership to raise our financial life up to the Divine Standard?

The answer is to develop certain attributes in consciousness. The first attribute is to *be aware of the Holy Self within as the Source and Absolute Cause of our supply*. This brings the Law into our consciousness—and our consciousness becomes the Law of Supply. The Master Thought of the 40-Day Prosperity Plan in *The Abundance ·Book*[2] is: "My consciousness OF God AS my supply IS my supply." Thus our consciousness becomes the law of supply unto us. The energy flows into manifestation through us, forever reproducing the tone, pitch and shape of our consciousness in the world of form. The main thrust of this Master Thought is to enable us to work with the higher law—the Law of Abundance—rather than the law of lack, because consciousness is fulfilling itself as law regardless of where it is focused. You can see why this attribute is so vital in the entire creative process.

The second attribute deals directly with the Third Aspect of the Trinity, so we must look at a combination of the primary terms used to describe the Holy Spirit: "Active Intelligence and Inspiration." In breaking down the definitions of these words we see an attribute of consciousness that represents *an alert, energetic, and imaginative state of mind with the incentive, stimulation and motivation to create.* This is the "vibratory tone" of the Third Aspect as described from a finite point of view, and it is this state of consciousness that we must have if we are going to be the proper channel for the Creative Force.

The third critical attribute is *sexual affinity with the Creative Energy of Spirit*, the all-providing substance. Do not be thrown by "sexual affinity." The word origin of affinity means "kinship by marriage, as distinct from blood kinship." In modern terms it means "a relationship united by mutual love and attraction." When an affinity is prefaced by sexual, the meaning is "an excited, enthusiastic, amorous, sensuous relationship drawn together by mutual love and attraction." This is the kind of natural affinity that we must have with the Creative Energy to insure that the consciousness-channel remains open and clear for the Divine Expression.

The fourth quality of consciousness is *a recognition of the need* and asking that it be met. If we deny that the lower nature (personality) has a need—in this case, money—we are limiting the manifestation process. But this is not registered in consciousness as a desperate, heavy, fearful need. It is rising up to a level above the lower nature and simply recognizing a hole to be filled for the benefit of the physical sense of being, a job to be done, an action to be taken. And the asking is really nothing more than an acknowledgement that the Self I AM already has everything and is even now bringing it into visible form.

And the fifth consciousness ingredient is *creative imagination*. Every successful school of thought since the beginning of the sacred academies has stressed creative imagination as a major key in clearing a path through consciousness for Spirit—"to clean the instrument." What do you see? What *can* you see from the highest vision? Can you not imagine streams of rich golden substance radiating through you and flooding your world with abundance? Can you not imagine money being attracted to your Magnetic Center from all points of the universe? Can you not, in your imagination, see *having* instead of lacking, an all-sufficiency instead of insufficiency? Use your imagination to clear the channel and keep it open!

Think of these attributes and begin to work with them daily in a program of *simultaneous action*. Meditate on the Truth that your consciousness of the inner Presence AS your supply IS your supply and work with the Higher Law of Abundance. Take on the active, inspired, energetic vibration of the Third Aspect of Divinity, and develop an excited, amorous and sensuous relationship with the Creative Energy flowing through you. Recognize the needs of your lower nature and be the Christ by giving what is needed as you release each demand to Spirit to be fulfilled easily and effortlessly. And use your creative imagination to see only fulfillment and a continuous all-sufficiency. When the attributes are active at once and working together, you are truly cooperating with "the fullness of the Godhead" individualized as you. You have become an ideal channel for the extension of Heaven into Earth.

Let us remember that in truth we are Fourth Dimensional Spiritual Beings expressing through consciousness in the third dimensional world of form and experience. Our work is to bring the Fourth Dimension into the third, and in doing do we cannot forget the visible, formed, manifest expressions of Spirit, including money.

We are not of this world but we are in it, so let's get back on track with the abundance that is already ours—not only for our personal needs but also to share and to use in the healing and harmonizing of Planet Earth.

A Meditation

I know that until the Realization Experience occurs, my purpose as a personality is to be consciously aware of the Divine Consciousness within, the Holy Master Self I AM in Truth. In the silence and stillness of my being, I am now aware of this Blessed Sacredness and I feel the Presence flooding me with Light.

This Great Self I AM is being, doing, and having everything now through my recognition of Its glorious Being. So this day I give up trying to make something happen and I place my total dependence on the Reality within. I trust this Master Self, and I am kept in perfect peace as I keep my mind stayed on the God-Being I AM.

Through my recognition of the only Cause and the only Source within, I become in tune with the Higher Law of Abundance. I am now conscious of the Inner Presence as my Supply. My consciousness of God as my abundance is my abundance, and with this understanding my consciousness becomes the law of abundance unto me. I understand. I know.

I feel alive all over and energetic throughout my being. I am vitally alert and wonderfully imaginative. I am highly stimulated and totally motivated, and I work with divine inspiration to be a clear and clean channel for the Creative Force pouring through me.

I feel this dynamic flow of Energy, and I love what I feel. The radiation is warm and sensuous. There is a deep mutual love and attraction as this bright golden substance, the creative thread of the Universe, moves easily and effortlessly through the eye of the needle I am, weaving the rich fabric of my life. It goes before me to reveal the reality of continuous abundance and prosperity everywhere present.

I rise above the level of the lower nature now and look below. I recognize what appears to be needs on the third dimensional plane, and I acknowledge that those needs are now being fulfilled by the Activity of Spirit. That which I AM and HAVE is coming forth into visibility in the phenomenal world.

I see it happening. The streams of Creative Energy are flowing mightily, flooding my life and affairs with abundance. The Light of God has completely illumined my world, and the darkness of lack and limitation has been dispelled. I see this clearly with my inner vision. And I behold this invisible Essence coming forth into visibility now and being attracted to the Magnetic Center I AM.

The Energy of Love has manifested as money and every other good thing, and all that I could need or want is rushing to me now. Everything that I see is Spirit made manifest, energy in form, therefore everything is spiritual. And I accept all the Good in the name of I AM, for the fullness of all belongs to the Master Self within. Now every question is answered, every problem solved, every need fulfilled. . .as it was in the beginning.

CHAPTER FOURTEEN

Five Principles of
Abundance

These principles can be utilized with miraculous results if
the attributes in the previous chapter are first developed
and working in consciousness—then the principles
become extensions of the attributes themselves. So let's
consider the attributes and the principles as "one following
the other" in the natural order of consciousness, all
working together in the process of creative cooperation.

We understand that everything is energy—omnipresent, infinite, undivided—constantly flowing
through us. And while the impersonal force does not
recognize our human conditioning factors, the Active Intelligence of Spirit does—and it seeks to help us function
as proper channels without violating the principle of free
will. The maximum pressure and rate never diminishes,
yet due to our self-imposed blocks Spirit moves through
individual consciousness in a rhythmic process much like
the ebb and flow of a tide. It exerts pressure on our points
of opposition to stimulate our awareness of the possibility
of a higher order of living (the knocking on the door in Rev.
3:20), then relieves the tension to allow us the opportunity
to consider our choices. This rhythmic beat and cyclic
vibration continues until we exercise our free will to open
the door and consent to be, as Edgar Cayce put it, "a

perfect channel through which the will of the Father may be done."[1]

This is where these five principles come in—to help us condition consciousness to be in greater alignment with the will and purpose of the Infinite, to choose for God, and to be receptive to the outpouring of the magnificent gifts that are ours by right of inherent possession. There are other principles that certainly apply, but these particular five have been tested with proven results.

Abundance Principle No. 1: *The Principle of Conscious Worth*

To grasp the significance of this principle let's remember that *God* is our Supply. The Presence, the Energy, the Substance, the very Existence of God is our Supply. God is all there is, and we can never be separated from God, so at this very moment we have the unlimited Resources of the Universe—right where we are.

Pause now and feel and see with your mind's eye the infinite Ocean of God-Energy that is everywhere present at once. At the very center of this omnipresent Creative Energy see a circle of light. This circle represents *you* as a Conscious Being, infinite Spirit individualized. Recognize that the Light, Force, Power, Energy, Substance, Life— both outside and inside the circle—are identical. There is no separation, nothing is divided, all is the same. The circle of light simply represents the Infinite being aware of Itself at a point of Self-Awareness. Therefore, *your* very existence, *your* essence, *your* life force, *your* energy is one and the same as the Infinite Presence of God.

We have the Cause of all things, of all effects, within us. The Divine Consciousness of our Self is eternally causing all things. What we are seeing in our phenomenal world is how our lower vibration consciousness limits the Causing of Spirit. To stop limiting the Unlimited we must embody the Truth of Who and What we are and be aware of the Infinity of Supply that we are and have. The Unlimited Universal Treasure is ours now. . .it is what we are! All of the Supply that is, which is eternal, infinite and without end, is the right of all, given to all as the very Existence of all. We could not ask for more than we already have, for we have it all now.

This is the Truth of each one of us, but unless we recognize this Truth and *feel* it throughout our being, our vibration of consciousness will limit the effect. Conversely, the greater the feeling of the Truth of Abundance, the fewer limitations will be placed on the process of Causing. Think of it this way: The visible expression (effect) is in direct relationship to how "supplied" we feel. And this brings us back to that first principle.

Regardless of the amount of money that you think you need to bring your life up to the Divine Standard of Harmony, can you realize that you have that much and so much more—right at this moment—in the invisible Realm of Supply? You *are* this supply. . .this Supply *is* you. If the creative energy in a grain of sand was suddenly made manifest as paper currency, the entire planet would be smothered in a blanket of bills so high that all sunlight would be blocked out. So, if you were to pronounce a "worth" on the Energy of Supply that you are and have, and which is flowing through your consciousness at this moment, could you not say that its value infinitely exceeds the amount of money you need or desire? Absolutely! You are totally unlimited.

This principle can best be summed up in this manner: **"The Law of Supply always translates your Worth, as you feel it and intuitively know it, into visible supply."** What is the Energy of Supply flowing through you, *as you*, worth? Realize your True Worth and let the Worthiness of Self accommodate the desired manifestation. Know your Self as infinite Supply with infinite Worth and remove all conditions on Cause.

Abundance Principle No. 2: *The Principle of Attraction*

The Law of Attraction draws visible supply to us from those who wish to exchange money for our products and services, and from those who may wish to share their abundance with us. Putting this principle into words we would say: **"The Law of Attraction is set into motion through the magnetic vibration of Love in the individual and the group. The radiation of unconditional, universal Love becomes its own channel to attract and receive the highest form of good, including visible supply."**

In my experience I have found it difficult to move above the human affection-type love into the higher realm of Divine Love without discipline and dedication. That is because Universal Love is not "natural" to the human sense of being—but something that Jan received from Spirit during meditation helped me greatly in this regard. It said, "Just love **Me** and I will love through you."

By loving the Lord-Self first, and then letting the radiation of Divine Love pour through us to "all that is"—the Law of Attraction is set in motion. But we must continue being a channel for this love, or the magnetic vibration will begin to slow down, thus reducing its attracting power. Until the lower nature is completely transmuted, we must work consciously and constantly with this mighty Force of Love.

Abundance Principle No. 3: *The Principle of Sharing*

This rule can best be stated this way: **"To give unselfishly is to receive more than that which was given. All are one, everyone is your self. To give to another is to give to your self, yet the reaction is always greater than the action."**

This does not mean that the person or group that you share with is going to give back to you more than you gave. But it does mean that the Universal Process will expand your gift as it returns to you through other channels. That is simply how the law works, and it was a basic teaching in the ancient Mystery Schools.

In the Old Testament it is called "tithing"—the giving of a tenth to God's work. In the New Testament it is seen more as "sharing"—and in the world to come the Greater Laws of Tithing and the Higher Laws of Sharing will be the foundation for the economic system. Keep in mind that where you give must always come from the guidance of Spirit—through your intuition or flashes of inspiration—

and not from guilt-induced pleas for money. But give you must to stay in the flow.

Abundance Principle No. 4: *The Principle of Impulsive Energy*

"Impulsive energy" is the Energy of Ideas, those that are forcefully propelled through consciousness, involuntarily and spontaneously, in answer to a need. In essence, it is the energy of Divine Guidance in the form of an idea to be implemented on the physical plane.

The principle may be worded as follows: **"Divine Ideas come into receptive minds as an impulsive force. Each idea has its own worth, which is translated into visible supply when implemented."**

I discovered this principle many years ago and found that in terms of money each idea certainly did have its own worth. Ideas came through, were put into action, and the "yield" was in direct proportion to the idea's value. So Jan and I took great delight in working with the little and big ideas and watching how each sustained us on the physical plane with a certain amount of visible supply during a specific timeframe.

For example, during one particular lean time in our lives Jan was given the idea to create a line of women's skirts—each hand-painted as an original creation. While she did not think of herself as an artist and had not painted before, she followed the guidance and designed, painted, and sewed a beautiful collection without help from anyone (on the physical plane). Then she made the rounds of the boutiques and quickly sold all her samples with stacks of orders for more. When this idea had run its course another one was in the wings to take its place.

Abundance Principle No. 5: *The Principle of Creative Activity*

The truth involved in this principle is that the Universe is not complete without you and your particular contribution on all planes of existence—spiritual, mental, emotional, and physical. Most of the people on the spiritual journey contribute their light, love, and energy through meditation, practicing the Presence, thinking positive thoughts, and feeling the love and joy in the unity of all life. But we must not overlook our contributions to the physical-material world, and I am about to use a four letter word that may shock you. It is *work*.

Working for the joy of it is our way of being an instrument for the creative expression of God. And the wondrous thing about it is that we are *compensated* for letting Spirit fulfill Itself through us. Imagine that!

Here is how I would describe this principle: **"Visible supply comes to those who invest in the cosmic process through creative activity—not to make a living but to make a life—for life is not complete without work to contribute to the greater whole."**

Regardless of your age and situation there is something that you can do to share your talents and abilities for the benefit of others. In the Nature of Spirit there is no such thing as a "fixed income"—unless fixed by individual choice. If that is not your choice, find that which is yours to do, do it to the very best of your ability, and Spirit will surely compensate you for your efforts. Remember, the Universe is not complete without *your* participation.

Put the five principles together in your daily life and there is no way to escape prosperity on the physical plane. Ponder, contemplate and meditate on your True Worth until you have the Worthiness Experience in consciousness. Set the Law of Attraction into motion by radiating the love of your God-Self and loving unconditionally as you have never loved before, and work with the process daily until it is automatic. Under the guidance of your Holy Self begin to share your bounty regularly and systematically— on wings of love and a heart filled with joy. Be open and receptive to Divine Ideas, and when they come accept them and implement them for all their worth. And work for the joy of it as a channel for the Creative Expression of Spirit, knowing that whatever part you play will make a difference in the Universal Scheme of Things.

It is a 5-part Investment Plan with a guaranteed return.

A Meditation

I understand my true worth now. I had thought that I was a human being with a mortal mind subject to the trials and tribulations of this world. All of that is in the past, for I have come to my Self and have recognized that Self as the only Reality. And as the I AM THAT I AM, I could not ask for more than I already have. My Worth is infinite, for I AM in truth the Worthiness of God.

How could I not love and adore such Magnificent Completeness? I love my Wholeness with all my heart, with all my soul, with all my mind, with all my strength. I know that to love my God-Self is the greatest commandment because it is the greatest secret. It is the Law of Attraction, the very Will of God that brings and holds everything together for good. And so I pour in that love to my precious Self, and the reciprocal action of my Self flows out as Unconditional Love, becoming its own channel to attract and receive the highest form Good in the Universe.

Knowing that I now have everything, I can begin to share with great love and joy. I understand that there is only Oneness in the unity of Soul and Spirit, and as I give, I receive, and as I receive, I give. And the great Plan of God is fulfilled on Earth.

Being in tune with the Infinite I AM, I am open and receptive to Divine Ideas. I hear the still small voice guiding me and I intuitively know what to do. I respond with the specific action that I am led to take, knowing that. . .I work, yet not I, for it is Christ doing all things through me.

I now go forward as the instrument for the Creative Expression of God—not to make a living but to make a life—for life is not complete without work to contribute to the greater whole. I now let the Magnificent Spirit I AM fulfill Itself on Earth as me. I am inspired!

CHAPTER FIFTEEN

Tell Me About Yourself

If we found the representative man/woman of the collective consciousness of humankind and said, "Tell me about yourself," we might hear a personal profile sketched in this manner:

"I am a self-packaged, self-contained human being of a particular race and sex, living on Earth and trying to make the best of it with the cards I've been dealt. I am here as a result of a so-called lucky day or night when my mother and father made the connection for a spontaneous creation.

"As a child I was lonely, and even with billions of people on the planet I am still alone. Everyone is. We are all solitary people, here all by ourselves and single-handedly trying to manage through life. You really can't trust other people because everybody's looking out for number one. And if there is a God out there, he's too vague and abstract to really be of any help with my problems. Oh I do pray occasionally when nothing else seems to work, but it is all a hit or miss proposition—sort of like getting conceived. So I've got to rely on my own wits and do what I have to do to keep my head above water.

"And there never seems to be enough of anything. I work like hell to make a little money, then spend half my time trying to dodge creditors. I find a little success, but I always know what's just around the next corner. Relationships all end up being disappointments, and I continually have to put up with a lot of stuff from people who try to tell me what to do.

"One good thing though, I've learned to live with all my physical problems, and I do have days when I feel fairly good. But I know that one of these days I'll get stuck in the ground someplace with a piece of granite above me showing how many years it took me to get from cradle to grave.

"And going on to the Beyond doesn't sound like a trip to Disneyland either, particularly when you think about being called on the carpet and made to pay for all your mistakes. The whole ball game, whether played here or there, seems to be a no-win contest. But that's life, isn't it? No wonder we scream when we come into this world, and then do everything we can to keep from going to the next one."

When the individual man or woman who spoke these words awakens to *the Cosmic Whirlwind*, a totally new and different world will come into view. Pause for a moment now and study the diagram on the cover of this book.

The top portion represents the fullness of God expressed in the Universal Sonship. In the middle part the fiery, whirling, creative Energies begin to individualize, and then come forth as the Auric Egg of Individual Being. On the higher level there is total unity and oneness of Selfhood, one Universal Spirit-Self, where the idea of separation has never entered. In the individualization there is only the extension of this Oneness, with absolutely no possibility of disconnection or isolation, even though the lowest aspect of being (personality) appears to have a physical form. And as this dynamic Force is funneled into individual expression, it carries with it the fullness of Universal Being, *which means the absence of anything contrary to Divine Principles.*

What are Divine Principles? They are the Laws of God, which include unlimited abundance, creative fulfillment, loving and harmonious relationships, joyful interests, radiant wholeness, right knowing, perfect peace, and eternal happiness. Accordingly, scarcity, failure, discord, boredom, sickness, uncertainty, conflict, and sadness do not exist in the world of individual being. If they appear to be a part of our world, it is because we feel and believe as the representative person of the race mind feels and believes, and these thought-forms are projected on our life screen as made up images about ourselves. We began making our homemade movies when we thought that we were set apart from God and isolated in some strange land, without the possibility of reconnecting until "the end of time." So it was only natural to accept human problems under the circumstances. Thinking that we were separate from our Source, what else could we expect?

By meditating on the diagram of the Cosmic Whirlwind and truly understanding that we are the Universe individualized—that we are the Kingdom that has come on Earth—our consciousness will begin to shift from solitary confinement to all-inclusive freedom. And we will in time realize that every personal problem has disappeared. There is no alternative. The difficulties *must* vanish with the conscious awareness and identification with the Cosmic Whirlwind. That is simply the way it works.

Throw your whole being into that Force Field. Move into that figure of the person in the diagram and realize the Divine Continuity of "as above, so below." Feel the Divine Energies pouring through you at every moment and radiating out from you to reveal the New World of Peace and Plenty. As within, so without. And see your Good returning to you in a tidal wave of splendid forms, conditions, and experiences—and begin to live in the Divine Estate that has been yours since the beginning.

Now tell me about yourself, as a representative man or woman of the Kingdom of Heaven.

"I am empowered from on High, and truly there is nothing that I cannot do, be, or have."

Amen.

NOTES

CHAPTER ONE: *The Art and Science of Prayer*

1. *Metaphysical Bible Dictionary*, Unity School of Christianity, Unity Village, MO, 1931.
2. Fillmore, Charles, *The Twelve Powers of Man*, Unity School of Christianity, Unity Village, MO, 1930.
3. Holmes, Ernest, *The Science of Mind*, Dodd, Mean and Company, New York, 1938.

CHAPTER TWO: *Blessing All and Praying for Others*

1. Bailey, Alice A., *Discipleship In the New Age*, Vol. I, Lucis Publishing Company, New York, 1972.

CHAPTER THREE: *Understanding Spiritual Principles*

1. Quote from the Dead Sea Scriptures, English translation by Theodor H. Gaster, appeared in *Sons of Darkness, Sons of Light*, by Mary La Croix, A.R.E. Press, Virginia Beach, VA, 1987.

CHAPTER FOUR: *More Pointers On Principles*

1. Price, John Randolph, *The Superbeings* (mass market edition), A Fawcett Crest Book published by Ballantine Books, New York, 1988; (trade paper) Quartus Books, Boerne, TX, 1981.
2. The Quartus Society, the membership organization of The Quartus Foundation, provides an energy link with like-minded people throughout the world. For a complimentary copy of the *Quartus Report*, write to P.O. Box 1768, Boerne, TX 78006.
3. Millions of people around the world join in a simultaneous global mind-link each December 31st at noon Greenwich time. The purpose: to reverse the polarity of

the negative force field in the race mind, achieve a critical mass of spiritual consciousness, and usher in a new era of Peace on Earth. World Healing Day began in 1986, with over 500 million participants, and continues each year on the same date.

CHAPTER EIGHT: *Being Born Anew*

1. Bailey, Alice A., *Esoteric Healing*, Lucis Publishing Company, New York, 1953.
2. Hall, Manly P., *The Secret Teachings of All Ages*, The Philosophical Research Society, Inc., Los Angeles, CA, 1977.

CHAPTER NINE: *All the Good in Life is Natural*

1. The twenty-two archetypes are the causal powers within us that influence every activity in our lives. The author refers to these manifesting agents as "Angels"—and his book, *The Angels Within Us*, will be published by Ballantine Books in early 1993.
2. *World Goodwill Newsletter* (1992, No. 2), published by WORLD GOODWILL, 113 University Place, 11th Floor, P.O. Box 722, Cooper Station, New York 10276.

CHAPTER TEN: *Ten Steps to the Fulfillment of Your Desires*

1. Fox, Emmet, *The Mental Equivalent*, Unity School of Christianity, Unity Village, MO, 1971.
2. Fillmore, Charles, *Prosperity*, Unity Books, Lee's Summit, MO, 1967.
3. Holmes, Ernest, *This Thing Called You*, Dodd, Mead & Company, New York, 1948.
4. Goldsmith, Joel S., *Practicing the Presence*, Harper & Row, Publishers, New York, 1958.

CHAPTER THIRTEEN: *A Consciousness of Abundance*

1. Price, John Randolph, *The Planetary Commission*, Quartus Books, Boerne, TX, 1984.

2. Price, John Randolph, *The Abundance Book,* Quartus Books, Boerne, TX, 1987.

CHAPTER FOURTEEN: *Five Principles of Abundance*

1. *The Edgar Cayce Reader,* under the editorship of Hugh Lynn Cayce, Coronet Communications, Inc. and Constellation International Publishers, New York, 1969.

BIBLIOGRAPHY

Emerson's Essays, Ralph Waldo Emerson, First and Second Series Complete in One Volume, Harper & Row, Publishers, New York; originally published by Thomas Y. Crowell Company, 1926.

Harper Study Bible, The HOLY BIBLE, Revised Standard Version, Zondervan Bible Publishers, Grand Rapids, MI.

The HOLY BIBLE, Authorized King James Version, The World Publishing Company, New York.

New World Dictionary of the American Language, Second College Edition, Simon and Schuster, New York, 1986.

The Quartus Report, monthly publication of the international Quartus Society, The Quartus Foundation for Spiritual Research, Inc., Boerne, TX.

The World Book Encyclopedia, Volume 6, ELECTRICITY, Field Enterprises Educational Corporation, Chicago, 1967.

A N
INVITATION

IN 1986, JOHN AND JAN PRICE GAVE A PARTY AND MORE THAN 500 MILLION PEOPLE SHOWED UP. THIS IS YOUR FORMAL INVITATION TO ATTEND THE NEXT GET-TOGETHER.
The first affair was on December 31, 1986, at noon Greenwich time, and was called World Healing Day, and World Instant of Cooperation. Regardless of the name, it was the first simultaneous global mind-link in history with people in all 50 states and 77 countries joining in—and the gathering was so successful that it has been repeated each year since.

In recognition of the event, John and Jan were invited as keynote speakers at the World Peace Symposium and the World Peace Center. Religious Science endorsed the concept and *Science of Mind* Magazine continually expands the guest list by featuring World Healing Day in each December issue. Unity had such high expectations that the Association of Unity Churches gave the Prices "The Light of God Expressing Award" in 1986. The Association for Research and Enlightenment encouraged its worldwide membership to participate in this "Bond for Peace"—and more that 500 other organizations did the same. The International New Thought Alliance saw the results, and in 1992 the Arizona District named John the recipient of its Humanitarian Award. *And you are cordially invited to be a part of this history-making event each December 31st, wherever you may be.*

A further word about the author

With Jan's collaboration John has authored more than ten books. His first one was *The Superbeings* published in 1981, which even a *business journal* (Texas) reviewed: ". . . this author is not some mountaintop guru mouthing vague platitudes . . . he communicates in a down-to-earth tone resembling a fireplace chat with a friend." When John wrote *A Spiritual Philosophy for the New World* nearly ten years later, "The Book Reader" wrote in its national review: "Price has written a wowser of a book without the usual runarounds—Practical to a T."

John and Jan have teamed up as guest lecturers at conferences sponsored by A.R.E., INTA, Religious Science, and Unity. They also hold frequent workshops and conduct an annual Mystery School on Walter Starcke's Guadalupe River Ranch near Boerne, Texas, where their Quartus Foundation for Spiritual Research is headquartered.

For information on membership in the international Quartus Society, and on books and tapes written and produced by John and Jan, please contact **The Quartus Foundation, P.O. Box 1768, Boerne, Texas 78006-6768. Telephone (210) 537-4689.**